The Responsibilities of Company Directors

Second Edition

Financial Times Management Briefings are happy to receive proposals from individuals who have expertise in the field of management education.

If you would like to discuss your ideas further, please contact Andrew Mould, Commissioning Editor.

Tel: 0171 447 2210
Fax: 0171 240 5771
e-mail: andrew.mould@ftmanagement.com

MANAGEMENT BRIEFINGS

GENERAL MANAGEMENT

The Responsibilities of Company Directors

Second Edition

ANDREW SPARROW

FINANCIAL TIMES
MANAGEMENT

FINANCIAL TIMES
MANAGEMENT
LONDON · SAN FRANCISCO
KUALA LUMPUR · JOHANNESBURG

*Financial Times Management delivers the knowledge,
skills and understanding that enable students,
managers and organisations to achieve their ambitions,
whatever their needs, wherever they are.*

London Office:
128 Long Acre, London WC2E 9AN
Tel: +44 (0)171 447 2000
Fax: +44 (0)171 240 5771
Website: www.ftmanagement.com

A Division of Financial Times Professional Limited

First published in Great Britain 1996
Second edition 1998

© Andrew Sparrow 1996, 1998

The right of Andrew Sparrow to be identified as author
of this work has been asserted by him in accordance
with the Copyright, Designs, and Patents Act 1988.

ISBN 0 273 63780 0

British Library Cataloguing in Publication Data
A CIP catalogue record for this book can be obtained from the British Library.

10 9 8 7 6 5 4 3 2 1

Typeset by Boyd Elliott Typesetting
Printed and bound in Great Britain

The Publishers' policy is to use paper manufactured from sustainable forests.

About the author

Andrew Sparrow LLB (Hons) is a specialist in corporate law and has a wide experience in commercial legal matters. He is Lead Partner, Corporate Services Department at Cartwright & Lewis Solicitors in Birmingham. He qualified as a Solicitor of the Supreme Court in 1989 and an early interest in industry and commerce attracted him to commercial law. He spent the period following his qualification working at one of the country's leading national groups of legal firms and took up his current position in 1992.

Mr Sparrow has published a number of legal papers and spoken at many seminars on a wide variety of corporate legal subjects. He has written and appeared in several television programmes aimed at training the legal profession in England and Wales and commented on legal developments on the radio.

He has a particular interest in the role of company directors and the legal status of directors. If you would like further details on any matter contained in this book, please contact Andrew Sparrow at:

Cartwright & Lewis Solicitors
2nd Floor
Wates House
100 Hagley Road
Edgbaston
Birmingham
B16 8LT

Tel: 0121-452 1989
Fax: 0121-452 1021

This book cannot be a substitute for specific advice and anyone contemplating important management decisions should take further advice.

Contents

Foreword

Sir Adrian Cadbury

Andrew Sparrow has filled an undoubted gap in the literature on boards and directors. One of the issues to which the corporate governance debate has drawn attention is the uncertainty of directors as to the precise nature of their responsibilities. There has been, for example, confusion as to the respective duties of directors and auditors in relation to financial reporting.

One reason for this uncertainty was that directors had no single source to which they could easily turn for an outline of the broad sweep of their responsibilities. As Andrew Sparrow points out, the duties of directors derive both from formal legislation and from case law. This makes the pulling together of the threads of their responsibilities complex and means that the legal position of directors is continually evolving.

This book will be particularly helpful to directors of smaller companies – the great majority – and indeed to those on the boards of bodies other than companies. It will alert them to the matters on which they would be wise to seek professional advice. It also deals usefully with such undiscussed, but by no means unusual, problems as dissent on the board. Finally, I believe that this book will encourage directors to recognise the need for them to keep up to date with the increasingly demanding nature of their duties.

1

Introduction

1.1 'The business of book learning'

All of us engaged in business, no matter of what kind, are closely associated with the prevailing economic climate. Every business is susceptible to the ebbs and flows of the domestic and international economy and despite the best endeavours of those responsible for the running of the concern, that business is necessarily exposed.

In today's volatile business world it is essential for managers to understand their responsibilities as directors of limited companies under the law. This area has been the focus of much recent litigation and it does not take much to find yourself in trouble with the courts. An understanding of such responsibilities will assist in the efficient running and development of the business.

The position of a director is the most important office within a limited company. The directors, either individually in the case of a sole director or collectively, are responsible for governing the affairs of the company and for running the business for which it was formed. Directors are charged with responsibility for adhering to the statutory and common law rules attached to their office.

Like the day-to-day hive of industry, company law does not stand still. The law in relation to directors is constantly in flux and the education of managers is not just desirable for its academic value, it is essential as a route to success in business.

Folklore dies hard and none more so than the belief that all successful businesses involve self-made individuals who, what they lack in formal education, make up with unbridled determination and intuitive business acumen. This may be true of some businesses, but not all, and even those happy few who possess this spirit can gain from an appreciation that the business of book learning should form a part of the business which they are empowered to run.

Wellington may or may not have said that Waterloo was won on the playing fields of Eton. It is submitted that today the economic battle will, in part at least, be won in the boardrooms of public and private companies of this country – that is if directors recognise the importance of their role and its impact upon the success of their company. The law will not tolerate clear abuse or neglect. The position of director is a privilege. It can also be a petard.

Directors tend to lead busy and reactive lives. This book is intended to serve as a succinct and orderly ready source of reference for directors of both public and private companies and to give practical assistance to the busy working company director. Over 300 questions are asked and answered.

1.2 How to use this book

I suggest that the best way to use this book is simply to read it through to the end, since in this way a general idea of the overall scope of a director's duties will be obtained. You should then keep it for reference, and refer to individual parts when the need arises. There are brief checklists at the end of each chapter to remind you of your broad responsibilities. The book is not a complete guide to English law on this subject. The object is to give the reader a broad outline and so provide guidance in the right direction.

The book is principally aimed at those directors whose experience of legal issues is relatively limited. It is also hoped that more experienced directors will be able to hone their existing knowledge using the questions outlined in the text.

In summary, this book helps you manage your company.

1.2.1 The sources of law

There are two principal sources of present day law: legislation and case law. Legislation is of course the term applied to Acts of Parliament or the law made under the authority of an Act. The other principal source of law is case law or judicial precedent, whereby judges are bound to follow rules of law established in previous court decisions. Even where legislation covers a particular aspect of the law, case law will build up concerning the interpretation of the legislation. In this report you will see notes at the ends of chapters with the name of a case or perhaps a statutory provision (for example, Company Directors Disqualification Act 1986, s 13). The purpose of that reference is to show the source of the legal statement to which the note relates.

1.2.2 The memorandum of association

There are many references to the company's memorandum in this book. Your company's memorandum is the document which outlines your company's constitution and defines the scope of your company's powers. It is in effect your company's charter and regulates its relationship with the outside world. It is filed with the Registrar of Companies on the company's incorporation and may be inspected by any member of the public.

1.2.3 The articles of association

There is also constant mention in this book of the company's articles, and in particular reference to Table A. The articles contain the internal regulations for the management of the company's affairs. They govern the rights of the directors and shareholders among themselves and set out the manner in which your company must conduct its affairs. Table A is simply a set of model articles found in the Companies (Tables A to F) Regulations 1985. Your company may have adopted Table A instead of registering its own articles, or it may specifically exclude Table A and set out its own articles. The third alternative is for a company to set out its own articles and adopt part of Table A. If your company's own articles are silent on a particular point, the appropriate provisions of Table A will apply unless it is stated that Table A has been specifically excluded. Usually some modification of Table A is found to be necessary and companies often modify provisions as to directors' rights and quorums to suit their own circumstances. All the major Companies Acts since 1862 have contained a model set of articles in the form of Table A. The Table A which applies to a company is the Table A in force at the date of the company's incorporation. The current Table A is the 1985 edition and copies of the standard Table A are widely available from law stationers.

1.2.4 The Registrar of Companies

In this book you will see on occasion reference to the Registrar of Companies who is based at Companies House.[1] The role of Companies House has been established in statute for a century and a half to incorporate companies and to assist in the provision of informed markets for the advancement of commerce by gathering and relaying information on these companies.

Companies House has the public records of over a million companies. Specifically, its main statutory functions are to incorporate and dissolve companies, to examine and hold documents under the Companies Acts and related legislation, and to make this information available to the public. Every limited company has a legal obligation to provide Companies House with an up-to-date annual return (which includes the registered office address and directors' and shareholders' details) (*see* section 5.5) and in most cases annual accounts.

There are 1 103 432 companies on the live register at Companies House.[2] A large number of these will have only two shareholders – perhaps a husband and wife or father and son, or perhaps two people who previously had worked together elsewhere.

In Great Britain in the year 1997 to date over 734 981 sets of company accounts have been filed with Companies House. In addition over 2 068 365 other documents required by law to be filed have been received and in excess of 167 715 new companies have been incorporated. The increasing popularity of incorporation shows no sign of slowing down, and Companies House projections for 1997–98 are that for the first time incorporation figures will hit the 200 000 mark.

This second edition has been fully updated and represents a statement of the law as it stands in April 1998.

Notes

1   Companies House, Crown Way, Maindy, Cardiff CF4 1UZ.

2   Companies House (1998) *The Register*, No. 36, Spring.

2

Appointment of directors

A company of course is an artificial body and can only operate by its human agents, which means you and your fellow directors. The articles of the company invariably provide that the business of the company shall be managed by the directors who will act collectively as a board.

2.1 Who is a director?

It must be noted that the Companies Act 1985 does not define a 'director' and the only assistance given is a note in s 741 that a director includes any person occupying the position of director by whatever name called. One must therefore look at the actual essence of the relationship and the role of the person in determining whether a person is or is not a director.

There are three types of director:

- **The executive director**

  This is the most common category of director. It refers to those who are involved in the day-to-day management and running of the company and are formally appointed to the board of directors. It is highly likely that this is the position that you occupy in your company.

- **The non-executive director**

  These are people who are involved with a company for perhaps only 15 to 20 days per year but who bring outside knowledge, experience and expertise to the position. There is no legally defined period for involvement. The increasing importance of the role of the non-executive director and their heightened responsibilities under the law is reflected in the Cadbury Report, the Greenbury Report and the Hampel Report (*see* section 4.10).

- **The shadow director**

  This is a person under whose directions or instructions the directors of the company are accustomed to act. You must take care if you appoint a shadow director because primary responsibility will always lie with the executive director. A common example of a shadow director is a parent company which may find itself in the position of shadow director of its subsidiary when the level of control which it exercises is such that the directors of the subsidiary are accustomed to act in accordance with its directions or instructions. It will always be a question of fact in each case as to whether this level of control exists.

What is the current test whether I am a shadow director?

There must be 'a pattern of control' exercised by you.[1]

If I control one director am I a shadow director?

No. In order for you to become a shadow director of the company, it is not sufficient that one of the actual directors is accustomed to act in accordance with your instructions. Unless the whole board, or at the very least a governing majority of it, is accustomed to act on your directions, you will not be a shadow director.[2]

There is another form of director which may be provided by the articles and this is the 'alternate' director. Such a director is appointed by a director and is entitled generally to perform all the functions of his or her appointer as a director in their absence.

I have heard the role of non-executive directors discussed in the media. Why is this?

Not every company has non-executive directors but there has been a campaign for the increased use of non-executives, particularly in public companies. The campaign had its origins in the Cadbury Report and continues today. Evidence of this is the recommendation that non-executives scrutinise the remuneration of executives as recommended by the Hampel Report.

The purpose of the campaign is to promote an independent view of the board's deliberations to help provide the company with effective leadership and ensure high standards of financial probity on the part of the company.

What is a de facto director?

This is somebody who acts as though they were a director in their day-to-day activities but who is not in fact a director appointed to the board. This is a dangerous position because in some instances the law treats a *de facto* director as an executive director with all the attendant liabilities. For example, the disqualification penalties may be applicable (*see* section 11.1).

Where should I look to find the procedure for the appointment of a director?

English law gives you almost complete freedom in terms of the machinery to appoint, but the answer is usually found in the articles (*see* section 1.2.3). The articles invariably delegate the power to appoint to the shareholders in general meetings.

2.2 Appointment of first and subsequent directors

There are two forms of appointment to consider:

- **Appointment of first directors**

  If you wish to register a brand new company you must provide a statement of particulars for the first directors of the company with the memorandum to the Registrar of Companies (*see* section 1.2.4). Your company cannot be registered without this statement. The statement must be in the prescribed form, it must be signed by or on behalf of the subscribers, and it must contain a consent signed by each person named in it as director to act as such. Upon incorporation, the people named are deemed to have been appointed the first directors and therefore the new company is born with a ready-made board.

  It is important for you to note, however, that any appointment made by the articles but not mentioned in the statement is void. In other words, that person will not be a director of the company.

- **Appointment of subsequent directors**

  Once your company is a going concern, the appointment of any new directors is once again governed by the articles.

2.3 Typical provisions governing appointment

What are the typical provisions found in the articles?

- It is usual when appointing a person to fill a vacancy or as an additional director for an ordinary resolution (*see* section 7.2.2(e)) to be passed by the company. Thus only a simple majority of shareholders entitled to vote and who do vote at a general meeting of the company is required. However, you should check that the articles do not allow loaded voting rights on this question of appointment in favour of a person or class of persons.

- A director may also be appointed by written resolution signed by all the shareholders, and if so there is no need for a meeting (*see* section 7.2.2(g)).

- There may be restrictions on the right to appoint. To prevent a shock appointment, your articles will normally require the proposed directors to sign a consent form and for the shareholders to sign a proposal which will then be left with the company for not less than 14 and not more than 35 days before the meeting. The minimum period of notice for proposed appointments is seven days for listed companies. In order to avoid members of a public limited company (plc) having to decide the appointment of all directors or, alternatively, none at all, there is an additional restriction which forbids two or more directors being appointed by a single resolution unless unanimously agreed by the meeting.

- The articles may also give you and your fellow directors sole power by majority vote to fill casual vacancies or add to the board.

  This is very useful but the maximum number must not exceed that specified in the articles. Such directors are not counted in the number of directors who retire by rotation in the usual way. Such an article must also make it absolutely clear that the shareholders' power has been removed.

What is a 'casual' vacancy?

A 'casual vacancy' is a short-term position. It does not include filling vacancies caused by those retiring by rotation or those whose term of office has expired. A vacancy caused by retirement by rotation has normally to be filled by the annual general meeting (*see* section 7.2.1).

2.4 Minimum and maximum number

How many directors must there be?

A private company need only have one director whereas a public company must have at least two. However, the company can by ordinary resolution from time to time increase or reduce the number of directors and prescribe a maximum and minimum number or both. Setting a maximum and minimum number is probably unwise as it only causes a stumbling block when adhered to and makes a mockery of the articles when ignored.

I am the only director in a private company. Can I also act as company secretary?

No, for the reason that one-man management is viewed unfavourably by the courts.

Can I assign my position as director to another?

Yes, if authority is given in the articles or by agreement to assign with another person, but in each case the assignment is of no effect until approved by special resolution of the company (*see* section 7.2.2(e)).

I am director of a private company. Can I nominate my successor?

Yes, if there is power so to do in the articles. You will not require sanction by special resolution of the company if it is clear that this power exists without a shadow of a doubt.

2.5 Age limit

Is there an age limit for directors?

- **Public company**

  Unless the articles state otherwise, a person aged 70 or more cannot be appointed as a director of a plc or of a private company which is a subsidiary of a plc unless the appointment is approved by the company in a general meeting. Anyone attaining 70 must retire unless his or her retention is approved in general meeting.

- **Private company**

  If yours is a private company there is no age limit and you can hold office as director if under 18 or over 70.

2.6 Managing directors

You may appoint a managing director to your board. The managing director has no specific powers given to him or her by law. The managing director's powers are based entirely on the terms of the delegation by you and your fellow directors as a board, and any service contract given to him or her. Most articles will allow the appointment of a managing director (*see* section 3.6).

What are the responsibilities of a managing director?

These will vary from one company to another. On the one hand the managing director may just be one of a team of executive directors with responsibility for the day-to-day running of the company's affairs, as distinct from, for example, the finance or sales director's role. Alternatively the title managing director may represent the most senior management post in the company. There is no definition under company law given to the role of managing director.

Article 72 of Table A allows you as a board to delegate 'such of your powers as you consider desirable' to a managing director. There is therefore a good deal of flexibility in the portfolio of powers which you may confer.

Checklist: Appointment of directors

1. • Are you or the individual you appoint to be an executive, non-executive or shadow director?

   • Do you understand the role of each, and what a *de facto* director is?

2. Appointment of first directors

   • You must provide a statement of particulars of first directors to Companies House containing consents to act duly signed by each first director.

   • Anyone not mentioned in the statement is not validly appointed.

3. Appointment of subsequent directors

   • This is usually by ordinary resolution or written resolution.

   • Check any restrictions in the articles on the right to appoint.

   • Do you know what a casual vacancy is?

   • Consider the minimum and maximum number of directors and any age limit.

4. Managing director

   • Is there authority to appoint a managing director in the articles?

   • What will be the managing director's responsibilities?

Notes

1 *Re: PFTZM Ltd* (1995) BCC 280.

2 *Re: Unisoft Group Ltd (No.2)* (1994) BCC 766.

3

Powers of directors – know your articles!

Where do my powers emanate from?

A company really acts through two bodies. One is the company in general meeting, i.e. the shareholders; the other is the board of directors. The board, as we have seen, is elected by the general meeting and is usually entrusted with the management of the company. There is no set range of powers at the disposal of company directors.

3.1 Powers contained in articles

Where do I look to find out if power is vested with me as a director?

As for other rules relating to the running of the company, you must look at the company's articles of association. You should make this your first task if newly appointed. This is because the relationship between the board and the general meeting is a contractual one based on the articles which will determine the extent of the powers conferred on the board. You should note that nowhere in the Companies Act does it say what directors may do.

Is management of the company normally delegated to the board of directors?

Yes, although it is open to a company to adopt whatever form of management it pleases. Most companies will adopt Art 70 of Table A which provides that:

> Subject to the provisions of the Companies Act, the Memorandum and the Articles and to any directions given by Special Resolution, the business of the company shall be managed by the directors who may exercise all the powers of the company.

In a company, neither the general meeting nor the board of directors is the ultimate authority. The authority is the company's constitution which is the articles.

Do I need to be formally appointed to the board to be considered a director?

No, not necessarily. The company must have directors whether it appoints them or not, and if you actually manage the business you will be occupying the position of director and regarded as such under the law (*see de facto* director at section 2.1).

3.2 Limitation of powers

Is the power given to directors to have a free hand in the day-to-day management absolute?

Not exactly. Remember – power corrupts, and absolute power corrupts absolutely. Therefore Art 70 of Table A permits interference by the shareholders if those holding a sufficiently large stake in the company feel strongly about a particular matter. A sufficiently large stake means enough to enable a special resolution to be passed, i.e. 75 per cent majority.

While the shareholders own the company, they cannot override the powers which, as a director, you have been given by the articles and they must yield to your authority. Moreover, shareholders cannot retrospectively reverse a decision taken by the board, even by special resolution.

It can be seen therefore that very little managerial power is retained by the company in general meetings.

Give me some examples of instances where my powers as director may be limited by shareholders.

- The Companies Act requires any increase in the authorised share capital of the company to be decided by resolution of the shareholders. Conversely, a reduction in share capital can only be carried out by special resolution (*see* section 7.2.2(e)), and then only with the consent of the court.

- Any alterations to the memorandum, such as changing the company name or its objects, or to the articles may only be done by special resolution of the shareholders.

- Remember, you may be removed as a director by an ordinary resolution of the shareholders unless the articles specifically give you weighted voting rights on this issue if you are also a shareholder (*see* section 10.2). The adoption of a service contract (which is considered later in this book), while not preventing your removal, will at least afford you a right to compensation in the event of removal (*see* section 9.3.1).

- The shareholders, as a means of protecting their position, may appoint Department of Trade and Industry (DTI) inspectors regardless of what the articles may say on this question. Shareholder protection is considered later at section 5.6. Similarly, the DTI of its own volition may appoint inspectors in circumstances again considered later (*see* section 6.3).

- Certain payments which you might receive as director are not in the hands of directors. These include compensation for loss of office, which must be approved by ordinary resolution, and payments in connection with a sale of your assets or shares.

The above are merely examples of restrictions on your powers but are not exhaustive and professional advice should be taken on other areas of interference.

My company has been incorporated as a limited company for many years. Will it necessarily have adopted Art 70?

No, as the current form of Table A came into effect only on 1 July 1985. Your company may not be using Art 70. Although the 1948 version which was the previous Table A contains a similar provision, it would be simpler to adopt the current version. As we have just noted, this must be done by passing a special resolution and filing it, together with a copy of the reprinted articles, at Companies House. The adoption of the latest Table A is recommended in any event as there are other differences between the old rules and the new. This book should be read as if the 1985 Table A were in operation in your company.

If your company predates the 1948 Companies Act on Table A, then once again consider alteration of the company's articles to bring them into line with current regulations.

Can simple changes be made to the articles of association without the need for a reprint?

Section 18(2), Companies Act 1985, says: '... the company shall send with it a printed copy of the Memorandum or Articles as altered.' A full reprint therefore may not be necessary. However, an amended version is.

3.3 Powers exceeded

Can the board, as a whole, commit the company to a transaction even if acting beyond its powers?

This is where the directors act *ultra vires* the company. *Ultra vires* means 'beyond the powers of'. The current legislation operates in favour of persons dealing with a company. If an outsider deals with the company in good faith – and they are deemed to act in good faith unless the contrary is proved – then the company will be bound by the transaction. This is so despite the board's lack of authority to enter into the transaction. It is binding without any need for ratification by shareholders in general meeting.

Can I bind my company if I act in excess of my authority?

This is where you act *ultra vires* the board. Here, the issue is whether the board did in fact authorise you to act at the extent of your authority. For an outsider to hold the company to a transaction where they have not dealt with the board but with you as an individual director, it is necessary for that outsider to show that you had authority, either actual or ostensible. Actual authority is clearly where you have been given powers under the articles or your authority is implied by the position you hold. Ostensible authority is that which appears to others. This involves your 'holding out' that you have authority. It is not enough merely that you have in fact no authority, you must give the appearance to that third party that you possess authority for that third party to compel the company to be bound by your actions (*see* section 3.6).

Simply, you and your fellow directors only possess those powers which the company itself delegates to you, and the company, for its part, cannot delegate powers to you that it does not have itself. Thus, if a particular activity is not permitted via an express or implied clause in its memorandum, then it is *ultra vires* and you and your colleagues may not engage in that activity.

3.4 Usual amendments to articles

I am a director in a private company. Can my company vary the provisions of the standard Table A?

Yes, your powers may be modified by an alteration of the standard Table A. The alterations made by most companies are generally similar and are achieved by the adoption of new clauses which have been prepared and used widely by law stationers (*see* section 1.2.3).

What are the usual alterations?

Here are a few examples:

- Most private companies simply give the board complete discretion over the transfer of shares. However, it may well be that you have firm and settled preferences as to where you wish your shareholding to end up following your departure from the company for whatever reason. Perhaps you may wish the value of your interest, which represents many years of hard work, to rest with members of your family.

- Alternatively, you may wish to give existing shareholders the opportunity to purchase your shares, thereby retaining the structure, balance and status quo of the company (*see* section 5.1).

- There may be a restriction on the number of shareholders which is not necessary as it is unusual to set a maximum number of shareholders.

- The standard Table A prevents you from voting at board or committee meetings on contracts or other matters in which you have a direct or indirect interest. This may be relaxed subject to certain overriding prohibitions imposed by statute (*see* section 4.8).

- Since the Companies Act 1989, it is not necessary for a company to execute documents with the aid of the company seal, but to avoid a possible challenge to the validity of a document, such as a lease, executed without the seal the articles should be amended to make it clear that the company seal is not needed.

Remember, powers are given to you; it is essential that they be used only for the purposes for which they were intended, and always in the best interests of the company.

3.5 The director's powers to enable the company to borrow

Can I as director exercise the borrowing power on behalf of the company?

Yes, most forms of articles will grant a specific power to directors to borrow. In addition there will usually be a power to secure that borrowing in a variety of ways.

What are the consequences of borrowing in the absence of specific power in the articles?

You may be liable both to the lender for breach of warranty of authority and to the company for breach of duty. Most lenders will, however, as a matter of routine, satisfy themselves as to the ability of the company to borrow and provide security when an account is opened or facilities granted. They do this by reviewing the memorandum and articles.

I know there is a requirement to file details of any charge, mortgage or debenture with Companies House within 21 days of its creation. Is this my responsibility?

Yes, registration is usually effected by the lender but the duty to file does in fact fall upon the company. It is essential that you register the charge in time. If the time limit is missed, what may have been a 25-year loan can become immediately repayable if, for example, someone buys the asset secured or an interest therein or a winding-up petition is presented to the company.

What should I do if I discover late filing of a charge?

The only remedy is to file late or amended particulars but this can still involve problems with rival securities in the event of one of the examples above arising.

Is there a specified form to be used when filing particulars of a charge?

Yes, Form 395. This is a standard form available from any law stationers. It is critical that you understand this duty to file particulars within 21 days. The consequences of failure are very great.

Can a lender to whom security has been given insist by means of a restriction on another form of borrowing being included in the articles?

Yes. The restriction may prevent further borrowing by, for example, invoice discounting or factoring, or hire-purchase or leasing arrangements.

The first step toward improved management is, therefore, **Know Your Articles**.

3.6 Powers exercised collectively

As a director you must appreciate that you may not have the same rights as, for example, a partner in an unincorporated business. The general rule is that you and your fellow directors must act collectively as a board.

Are there any exceptions to the general rule?

Yes, in practice most companies will delegate to certain members of the board specific tasks such as finance, marketing, etc. Most companies' articles will allow delegation, and indeed Art 72, Table A, gives a general power to do so.

Another typical exception to the general rule is the appointment of a managing director (*see* section 2.6). To the outside world and any trading partner your managing director will have 'ostensible' authority and so, even if not formally appointed as such, a director held out as managing director and as having the authority to bind the company will do so.

Similarly, a director held out as finance director will bind your company in relation to any financial dealings such as appointing financial advisers. Your company will be bound to any arrangements entered into if once again the director had ostensible authority (*see* section 3.3).

The reality is that in business one often deals with a single director and not just a managing or finance director. The assumption is usually that the individual has the authority to bind his or her company. However, you should remember that, although the law will on occasion use the 'holding out' argument to protect you when dealing with an individual from another company, this principal will apply with equal force to you and your fellow directors.

I have been charged with responsibility for a certain aspect of the company business, for example sales. What should I do to ensure proper authority?

First, you must be satisfied that the company's articles do allow delegation to an individual director. As we have seen, most do. Second, you should request your board to pass a resolution appointing you as sales director and ensure that the resolution is properly minuted (*see* section 7.1.4).

Checklist: Powers of directors

1. The articles define your powers.

2. The management of a company is usually delegated to its directors by the articles. Check your company has adopted Art 70, Table A.

3. Directors do not have absolute power.

   Do you know the instances where directors' powers are limited by shareholders?

4. A director can bind your company to a contract with an outsider, even if it is beyond the company's powers.

5. You cannot act beyond the authority given to you by the company.

6. Your company can resolve to change its articles in relation to the powers of directors by a 75 per cent majority vote of the shareholders.

7. Directors are usually given the power to borrow on behalf of the company.

   Check that details of any charge, mortgage or debenture are filed at Companies House within 21 days of their creation.

8. If appointed director with a specific area of responsibility, e.g. finance, sales, marketing, ensure your company's articles allow delegation to an individual and insist a resolution is passed and minuted at board level.

4

Duties of directors

4.1 To whom do you owe your duty?

You owe a duty to:

* your company;

* outsiders.

In this book we shall focus on your duty to the company.

4.1.1 The company

What is meant by my duty to the company?

As director you are both an agent and trustee of the company for which you act. You are an agent because the company itself cannot act in its own person, for it has no person; it can only act through its directors. Remember, the company is an artificial body, it is a legal fiction. You are the individual selected to manage the affairs of the company for the benefit of the shareholders. Second, you are a trustee. It is an office of trust, which, if you undertake it, it is your duty to perform fully and entirely. In essence you are a trustee of the company's money and property, and an agent in the transactions which you enter into on behalf of the company.

In this chapter, therefore, the legal duties which you owe to the company are outlined.

4.2 Good faith

Your duty is to act bona fide in the company's interest and to use your powers for the proper purposes for which they were given to you. This is a subjective test but with an objective threshold. You must exercise your discretion and powers honestly and sincerely in what you, and not what a court may, consider is in the company's interest. However, good faith is not in itself sufficient. If your act or decision is one which no reasonable director could properly have come to, the court may intervene.

Honesty is the best business policy you will ever adopt.

4.2.1 Proper purpose

What are proper purposes?

Your powers must be exercised for the purposes for which they were conferred and not for any 'collateral purpose', even if you honestly believe that you are acting in the company's best interest.

Give me an example of using my powers in my genuine belief for the company's interests but nonetheless improperly?

You might issue shares in an attempt to defeat a threatened takeover rather than for the prime purpose of raising capital. In this case there is no bad faith on your part but there is a breach of duty and this time the test is objective.

Your duty of good faith may be summarised by the paraphrasing of a famous court judgment which is instructive:

> If you act within your powers, if you act with such care as is reasonable to be expected from you, having regard to your knowledge and experience, and if you act honestly for the benefit of the company you represent, you will discharge your legal duty to the company.

4.3 Skill and care

What am I expected to do to promote the company's welfare?

You are not expected to be an expert in the type of business which the company promotes unless you are appointed as such in view of your specialist qualifications. Many boards consist of persons who are specialists in business administration, or in certain general aspects of business management such as legal, financial, accounting, banking or export trade practice. You are entitled to rely upon the advice of your fellow directors in matters in which they are, or should be, experts. In summary, it is a subjective test of skill. You need not exhibit in the performance of your duties a greater degree of skill than may reasonably be expected from a person of your knowledge and experience.

Might I be liable for errors of judgment?

Where you take part in the company's business, if you act honestly for the benefit of the company you represent you will have discharged your duty and should not be liable for a simple error of judgment. Mere imprudence or want of judgment is not negligence. There exists what is known as the 'business judgment' rule. This simply means that the courts are reluctant to evaluate the performance of management and to second-guess its decisions. You are not to be blamed, at least in law, if your management decision does not turn out for the best. Criticism of you is the task of the shareholders of the company, not the court.

However, the day of the incompetent amateur is over. There is now legislation in the form of the Company Directors Disqualification Act 1986 requiring disqualification of directors of insolvent companies where conduct shows them to be unfit to manage a company (*see* section 11.3.6). In addition, the Insolvency Act 1986 imposes personal liability on directors when they should have realised the company faced insolvency and failed to take steps to minimise the loss to creditors (*see* section 11.5). This legislation involves the courts in evaluating the quality of management decisions.

Remember, if you have a service contract with the company it may require you to satisfy an objective standard of reasonable skill and care which is higher than the law might otherwise have demanded.

Do I have to give continuous attention to the company's affairs?

No, your duties are of a periodic nature, to be performed at periodic board meetings. As a matter of law you are not required to attend all such meetings, although you ought to whenever you reasonably can. Certainly, effective commercial management will usually make regular attendance a must, and if you have a service contract it will usually require you to devote the whole of your working time to the company.

Can I rely on the opinions of outside experts?

Yes, you are entitled to rely upon the advice of an independent outsider, and indeed on some occasions you may be considered negligent if you proceed to a decision without first obtaining expert advice, such as legal advice. However, such an outsider must appear to be qualified to give such advice and upon receipt of such advice you must yourself exercise your judgment.

Can I rely on my co-directors and officers of the company?

The following offers some guidance on this question.

*   It is your duty as director to see that the company's monies are from time to time in a proper state of investment, unless the company's articles of association justify you in delegating that duty to others.

*   When presenting the annual report and balance sheet you ought not to be satisfied as to the value of the company's assets merely by the assurances of your chairman, nor with the expression of belief of the auditors (*see* section 5.7).

*   A list of cheques to be authorised by the board, whether or not already paid, should be presented at each board meeting showing the amounts and names of the payees. Obviously this is impracticable for large companies but even there you must follow the proper procedure for delegating powers under the articles. If you

so delegate you need not constantly supervise, but if there is anything which seems a bit odd, for example an unusual payee, a payee with whom – to your knowledge – the company does not do business, a payee known to be associated with a fellow director or officer, an unusually large amount or a cheque drawn at an unusual time, the very least you should do is enquire. Generally you can rely on the properly delegated subcommittee of the board or a relevant officer when there is no reason to call for an enquiry. Nonetheless you do have a duty to supervise and enquire into the conduct of the company's affairs, particularly where there are suspicious circumstances or other reasons for doing so, and failure may render you in breach of duty. You must accept that on occasions your duty to the company as well as your own interest require you to ask irritating and embarrassing questions. If you do have suspicions you should ask for an explanation. If you do this, and if you receive what appears to you to be a satisfactory answer, then you will have discharged your duty.

4.4 The interests of employees

Do I need to have regard to the interests of the company's employees when performing my function?

Yes, the Companies Act imposes this obligation upon you, but your duty is owed to the company and not to the employees, still less to any one employee in particular. So long as the company is a going concern, this omission to recognise employees in their own right as an object of your concern probably has little impact on company policy. This is because any decision to further the interests of the employees is likely to benefit indirectly the shareholders by creating a more contented workforce. In other words, the interests of your workforce may imperceptibly merge with, and become, legitimate commercial considerations of yours.

Unfortunately the law offers no guidance as to how you should strike a balance between the interests of employees in general as well as the interests of the shareholders of the company if they conflict. In this instance your business judgment will prevail and the courts will be reluctant to interfere (*see* section 4.3).

4.5 Nominee directors

I have been appointed nominee director by a parent company, shareholder, creditor, union or the workforce. Am I bound to act in accordance with the directions of my principal or appointer?

No, such action is unlawful. There is no such thing as a delegate director in English law. If you see yourself simply as a watchdog for those who put you on the board you will be guilty of a breach of duty. Remember, the law expects you to devote your loyalty to the company as a whole.

4.6 The interests of creditors

What is my duty to creditors of the company?

It has long been established that as a director you owe your duty to the company, and not to its present or future creditors as such. This is certainly the case where the company is solvent. In this instance the company owes a duty to its creditors to keep its property inviolate and available for repayment of its debts. The conscience of the company, as well as its management, is confided to you as a director. You do, however, have a general responsibility to creditors to ensure that the company's property is not dissipated or exploited for the benefit of yourself or your fellow directors to the prejudice of the creditors.

Does my duty alter if the company is insolvent?

Yes, if the company is insolvent your duty changes and instead of a general responsibility to creditors you must have a regard to their interests.

The terms of the company's line of credit give the creditor control over the company. Where do my responsibilities lie?

This situation might arise because your company has sought the assistance of a venture capitalist organisation. Your responsibility to creditors when your company is solvent as outlined above becomes blurred in this instance and the issue has yet to be determined by the courts. Commercial lenders usually require rights of control or participation in the company and there remains a question of how their interests must be properly characterised by you.

4.7 Personal or secret profit

As you are both an agent and trustee of the company it follows that you must not make a personal profit from your position beyond what you receive as authorised remuneration.

If you are in any doubt whether you should retain or account for profits or benefits you should seek the approval of an ordinary resolution at the company's next board meeting (*see* section 7.1). You would have to show full disclosure and rejection of an opportunity by the company to defeat an allegation of personal profit. Moreover, if you were involved in the board decision to reject, your burden of proof will be correspondingly greater. Indeed, there is an exception to the general principal that a director may keep his or her personal profit where it is ratified by the members in general meeting and this is where the directors are themselves in the majority and use their vote to pass the resolution.

4.7.1 Examples of personal profit

What if I receive fees from a subsidiary company?

If you are appointed to the board of a subsidiary or to some other position where you receive fees or benefits you are liable to account for them. However, your company's articles of association may allow you to retain your fees provided you have disclosed your interest. In these circumstances you must check the articles.

What if I receive profits after I retire?

Let us consider an example. You failed to secure a contract for the company but are then asked by the customer to perform the contract in your private capacity. You get yourself released from your service contract on the grounds of ill-health, and take up the contract. There is a clear conflict of interest as the opportunity to get the contract arose out of your position as director. If, however, you had vacated your office before receiving the approaches which led to the contract, the position would almost certainly be different. A more common situation is if you leave the company with little more than a general hope of obtaining the business which you later acquire. In this instance you may be able to retain profits subsequently earned.

What if the company does not wish to pursue further business with a customer?

If your main reason for resigning is your dissatisfaction with the company and if the company was at no relevant time in pursuit of further business from the customer there is no real opportunity which has been diverted from the company. However, if you resign mainly to seek business from a customer, or at a time when there was a real or imminent business opportunity for the company, your actions would be in breach of your duty not to make a personal profit.

4.7.2 Generally

If you used company assets to generate a business opportunity which the company is capable of exploiting commercially but which you then divert to yourself, you are liable to account to the company for any profits made.

4.8 Interest in contracts

Can I have an interest in a contract with the company?

You must not have a personal interest in a contract or other transaction with the company whether actual or proposed unless:

- First, you disclose it under s 317, Companies Act 1985, at a board meeting (*see also* section 4.8.1). This must be the first meeting at which the transaction is considered or the first meeting after you acquire your interest, whichever is the later.

- Second, the company's articles must permit your interests (*see* sections 3.4 and 7.1.2). The articles will usually allow such an interest subject to:
  - certain transactions which are unlawful or which are regulated under the Companies Act, for example property dealings or a loan or quasi-loan made by the company to you (*see* section 8.4);
  - your making disclosure to the board of the nature and extent of any material interest.

4.8.1 Notice of interest

How do I give notice of an interest?

You may give a general notice either:

- that you are interested in a specified firm or company; or
- that you are interested in any transaction between the company and a person connected with you, for example your husband or wife, children or stepchildren, or

companies in which you control 20 per cent of the voting rights or of the equity by nominal value. You must take reasonable steps to ensure that the notice is read at the next board meeting.

Can I give general notice that I shall have an interest in all dealings with XYZ & Co.?

Yes, provided the company's articles permit it. They usually do by adopting Art 86 of Table A, Companies Act 1985 (*see* section 1.2.3). Once again, check your articles of association.

Can I give disclosure informally by discussions before the board meeting?

No.

Can I vote or be counted in a quorum at a board meeting where my interest is being considered?

No, unless:

- you are being given an indemnity or security against company loans or obligations which you have taken on yourself; or

- the company is giving security to the third party in respect of such obligations; or

- your interest arises because you are taking shares or debentures in the company or any of its subsidiaries; or

- the business relates to a retirement benefit scheme approved or requiring approval by the Inland Revenue; or

- the company's articles allow the general meeting by ordinary resolution to suspend or relax the restriction; or

- where the company's articles expressly permit it.

What if the rule that I must not have an interest is contradicted by the articles?

This is unlikely, but if relevant you must get the contract approved by the members in general meeting. You can vote through your own shares in that general meeting provided it does not amount to a fraud on the minority shareholders (*see* section 5.6) or on creditors if the company has run into financial difficulties. The latter might involve a deliberate though not necessarily dishonest depletion of assets which the creditors were entitled to keep intact for their benefit. The courts, however, have generally refused to be involved in what they consider to be a scholastic or academic exercise.[1]

I am a director of a listed company. Can I vote at a board meeting where my interest is being considered?

No, the company's articles will exclude your right to vote where you have a 'material interest'. Any exceptions in the articles require the consent of the Council of the Stock Exchange.

What if I have failed to disclose my interest or not complied with the terms of the articles giving permission?

The contract does not become void but the company may rescind it if it is not too late to do so and you must account for your profits. However, where there has only been a technical breach with no deliberate concealment the rule is something of a 'paper tiger' and the courts will be reluctant to rescind a contract.

4.8.2 Further disclosure requirements

If I have disclosed my interest to the board, are there any further requirements upon me?

Yes, there may be certain matters which need to be disclosed by way of notes to the accounts of any financial year in which the transaction was entered into or was still in force.

Give me some examples of such transactions

- These are usually loans, quasi-loans and certain other forms of credit provided to you exceeding in aggregate £10 000 (*see* section 8.4.3). Alternatively, this may be the provision of security to you if you have already been given credit by a third party, or any agreement to enter into such an arrangement. The arrangement need not have lasted for the whole of the financial year.

- Any other transaction in which you have a direct or indirect material interest. It is in your fellow directors' judgment as to what is 'material' but the transaction must at least exceed £1000 and in other cases not exceed in aggregate £5000, or 1 per cent of the net assets of the company.

- Your director's service contract. While it need not be disclosed by way of notes to the accounts (but *see* section 8.5 on the Greenbury Report) it must be open to inspection by members except where your contract can be terminated without compensation within one year. Contracts in excess of five years must be approved by ordinary resolution of the shareholders (*see* section 9.3.1).

Do I need to notify the company of my shareholdings and other interests in the company's securities?

Yes, when you take office, and you must also notify any dealings in such shares or securities. This information will be filed by the company in its Register of Directors' Interests (*see* section 5.5) and will be open to public inspection by members of the company and by the public.

The law requires very detailed particulars of the disclosure you need to give of matters which must be noted in the accounts.

This includes, in the case of a loan or quasi-loan, the amount due at the beginning and at the end of the financial year, any arrears of interest and any provision made for default. In any other case, what the value of the transaction is must be disclosed.

All the members of my board know I have an interest anyway. Do I need to disclose the obvious?

Yes.[2]

Each member of the board is aware of each other's interests. Can we simply imply disclosure?

No.[3]

I am sole director of the company. Do I need to disclose my interest?

Strange as it may be, yes, you must still make a declaration and record it in the minutes.[4] To complete the unreality, although not in fact required, it only remains for you as sole director to pass a resolution of thanks to yourself!

4.9 Contracts with the company

4.9.1 The general rule

As a director you must not put yourself in a position where there is a conflict, whether actual or potential, between your personal interests and your duties to the company.

It follows that your powers of contracting with the company are extremely limited. This restriction is for a good reason. The company is entitled to the collective wisdom of its directors and if any director is interested in a contract, his or her interest may conflict with his or her duty. You are only allowed to enter into a contract if you make full disclosure of all material facts to the shareholders of the company who then approve the contract. This rule applies even if the contract is a fair one. The law will not enquire as to the merits of the agreement but will merely seek to ensure that the rule is being adhered to. The restriction is enforced by s 317, Companies Act 1985, which applies to all types of companies and cannot be excluded by the articles of association. The section and subsequent case law require you to disclose to your full board of directors any interest, direct or indirect, which you might have in a contract or proposed contract with the company. Such disclosure puts the other directors on notice to scrutinise the terms of the contract.

Provided, therefore, full disclosure is given you will not be required to account to the company for any benefit that you derive by reason of your director's interest. However, there are other restrictions imposed by Act of Parliament (*see* section 1.2.1) which regulate your dealings with the company. The following series of questions serve to identify those further restrictions on your freedom to contract with the company.

I wish to receive a loan from the company. Can I do so?

Generally no. However, a more detailed consideration of the issue of loans to directors is contained in section 8.4 later in this book.

May I buy property from, or sell property to, the company?

Yes, but the transaction is subject to the approval of the shareholders in general meeting.

I wish to receive a tax-free payment from the company. What is the position?

Such payments are prohibited and any agreement to make such a payment is treated as an agreement to pay the sum stated, but subject to deductions of tax. That is, as though the net sum were a gross sum.

Can the company pay me compensation for loss of office?

Yes, provided the payment is disclosed to and approved by the shareholders by ordinary resolution. The payment must also be disclosed in the accounts. Further detail upon compensation payments can be found in section 10.3.

I hold shares in the company or in a company which is part of the company's group. Do I need to disclose my interest?

Yes, the directors' report must disclose each director's interest in either case in shares at the beginning and end of the financial year (*see* section 5.7).

I am a director in a company which is on the Stock Exchange. May I deal in options?

No, such action is prohibited by the Companies Act 1985.

I have an interest in securities of the company or one of its associates. What must I do?

You must notify your interest to the company and it must be recorded in the company's register (*see* section 5.5.2). This is in addition to your general duty to disclose individual and group acquisitions of voting shares.

Remember, the principle of avoiding conflicts with personal interest needs to be borne in mind, particularly if you are a director of a small private company and especially if it is newly incorporated. The distinction between a one-person unincorporated business and a one-director company may not be immediately clear but you do not have the same liberty to withdraw profits from the company as you would have in an unincorporated business. Company profits belong to the company. The purpose of the duty to disclose to the board any direct or indirect interest you might have in a contract with the company in the case of a sole director is to give you a 'pause for thought', to remind yourself of the possible conflict of interest and of your obligatory duty to prefer the company's interest to your own.

4.9.2 Consequences of breach

What will happen if I breach my duties?

As a director you owe your duty to the company and it is the company which will bring an action against you for any loss resulting from breaches. Shareholders too may bring an action in their own name but on behalf of the company where the company cannot or will not sue and this is considered later in this book in section 5.6.

It is important to realise that proceedings may be brought against you if:

• you are a *de facto* or shadow director (*see* section 2.1);

• you are a retired director (*see* section 10.4);

• you are a bankrupt director (*see* section 11.3.5);

or against your estate if you have since died.

If you are in breach of your fiduciary duties and your duty of skill and care the company may:

- seek an injunction or declaration, for example where its own board is threatening to take some action beyond its powers or the powers of the company – that is, where there is a continuing breach;

- seek damages or compensation – you and all directors who participate in the breach are jointly and severally liable although there is a right of contribution from fellow directors;

- rescind contracts with the company provided that this is still possible and third-party rights have not intervened;

- seek an account of profits – if the profit arises out of a contract with the company, the company can normally claim an account of any profit made by you whether or not it rescinds the contract;

- obtain restoration of company property which is in your hands, including property it was your duty to acquire for the company;

- summarily terminate your service contract if your conduct amounts to grave misconduct (*see* section 9.3.11).

Most actions which can be brought against you are barred after periods of three or six years by the Limitation Act 1980 but these limits do not apply for fraud, fraudulent breach of trust or for the recovery of trust property which has passed through your hands.

4.10 The Hampel Report 1997

4.10.1 Background

In recent years a growing debate has emerged over the extent to which the board practices and procedures and financial reporting of this country's largest companies should be regulated. Against mounting dissatisfaction at the divide between directors' remuneration and the performance of their companies and to give greater clarity to the responsibilities of directors, a committee was set up in May 1991. The committee – under the chairmanship of Sir Adrian Cadbury – was established by the London Stock Exchange, the Financial Reporting Council and the accountancy profession. Its purpose was to recommend a Code of Best Practice which would promote the highest standards of behaviour and ethics. The Committee on the Financial Aspects of Corporate Governance produced its Report in December 1992. It become known as the Cadbury Report.

What is corporate governance?

The Cadbury Report defined corporate governance as 'the system by which companies are directed and controlled'. Your responsibilities and those of your fellow directors is to 'set the company's strategic aims, provide the leadership to put them into effect, supervise the management of the business and report to shareholders on your stewardship'.

4.10.2 The Hampel Report

The Hampel Committee on Corporate Governance under the Chairmanship of Sir Ronald Hampel, Chairman of Imperial Chemical Industries, was borne out of the recommendations of the earlier Cadbury and Greenbury Reports. The Committee was intended to review the implementation of the Cadbury and Greenbury findings. In December 1997 the Final Report was published.

What has been the approach taken by Hampel?

The Report marks a further stage in the maturing of the corporate governance debate started with the Cadbury Report. However, what is good for one company may not be right for another and the Hampel Report states that corporate governance is not an end in itself. The Report allows for different models and for different circumstances, and is not a straightjacket for all companies.

At the heart of the Report is the recommendation that once in the boardroom, all directors, whether executive or non-executive, should act as one body. That is not to say that they will not fulfil different tasks. As an executive director you have a responsibility to manage within the context of the strategy set by your fellow board members. Non-executive directors will often fulfil oversight roles as members of, for example, audit or remuneration committees. However, all directors, as a board, must take responsibility for the proper governance of your company's business.

Is the Hampel Report designed to streamline the corporate governance guidelines?

Yes. In response to many requests during the consultation process, the Hampel Report recommends the production of a set of principles and code which embrace Cadbury, Greenbury and the recommendations of the Hampel Report. It is, therefore, intended to produce a corporate governance 'bible' which will represent a single corporate governance guide. Once this document has been produced, it will be passed to the London Stock Exchange so that it can sit alongside the Listing Rules. It is then recommended that the London Stock Exchange issue the documents for consultation together with any proposed changes to the Listing Rules.

What are the principle recommendations of the Hampel Report?

- Every listed company should be headed by an effective board which should lead and control the company.

- The board should include a balance of executive directors and non-executive directors so that no individual or small group of individuals can dominate the board's decision taking.

- The board should be supplied regularly with information to enable it to discharge its duties.

- There should be a formal and transparent procedure for the appointment of new directors to the board.

- All directors should be required to submit themselves for re-election at regular intervals and at least every three years.

What in summary were the recommendations of the three corporate governance reports?

Cadbury

Established by the accountancy profession the Cadbury Committee reported in May 1992.

Chairman: Sir Adrian Cadbury, former Chairman of Cadbury Schweppes.

- Balance of power at the top of companies, preferably through separate chairman and chief executive.

- At least three independent, non-executive directors.

- Formal nomination and selection procedures for non-executives.

- Remuneration committees to set pay of executive directors.

- Maximum three-year contracts.

- Fuller pay disclosure for chairman and highest paid directors, expecially of bonuses.

- Audit committees to aid independence of auditors and ensure effective internal control.

Greenbury

Established by the CBI, the Greenbury Committee reported in July 1995.

Chairman: Sir Richard Greenbury, Chairman Marks & Spencers.

- Remuneration committee to report separately from the board.

- Details to include full pay and bonuses for each director including pensions.

- One-year notice periods the norm, two years the maximum.

- Greater emphasis on long-term bonus schemes rather than options and annual bonuses to be voted on by shareholders.

- Bonuses should be based on demand in performance criteria.

- Directors' pay increases should 'be sensitive' to pay rises elsewhere in the company.

Hampel

Formed to monitor the Cadbury and Greenbury codes the Hampel Committee reported in December 1997.

Chairman: Sir Ronald Hampel, Chairman ICI.

- Boards should assess directors' collective and individual performance.

- At least a third of the board should be non-executive.

- Non-executive directors can be paid in shares.

- Rejection of lighter rules for smaller companies.

- Rejection of shareholders' votes on directors' remuneration policies and packages.

- Rejection of compulsory voting by institutions.

- Separation of chairman and chief executive preferable but not essential.

One must bear in mind, however, that high standards of corporate governance promote confidence by the investing community and the public at large in the companies that practise them.[5]

4.11 Additional duties when also company secretary

All companies are required to have a company secretary but a sole director cannot also act as company secretary. However, in other instances you may act with dual capacity and if so will be subject to a number of additional duties. The company secretary is the chief administrative officer of the company. The directors rely on the expertise of the secretary to ensure that all administrative procedures are carried out in line with current legislation. It is a misconception to believe the role of the company secretary is an unimportant one required by legislation but serving no useful purpose. The Companies Act 1985 and most articles of association do not in fact specifically define the powers of the secretary to act on behalf of the company. However, the following areas are recognised as coming within the remit of the company secretary and are considered to be good business practice.

- **Board meetings and general meetings:** preparing agendas and notices (*see* section 7.1.1), notifying those concerned, attending and minuting decisions (*see* section 7.1.4) and ensuring that correct procedures are followed in line with company legislation.

- **Memorandum and articles of association:** ensuring that the memorandum and articles are complied with, that they are in line with current legislation and that correct procedures are followed both in making alterations and in the type of alterations made (*see* sections 1.2.2 and 1.2.3).

- **General compliance:** ensuring that all necessary returns are made under the Companies Act.

- **Statutory registers:** maintaining all statutory registers and retaining them at the registered office in a safe place (*see* section 5.5).

- **Share registration:** maintaining the Register of Members (*see* section 5.5.1), preparing the documentation to effect transfers, dealing with all communications in respect of shares and issuing documentation regarding allotment, capitalisation or other share information.

- **Registered office:** receiving and distributing all correspondence received by the company at the registered office and ensuring that relevant documents are available for public inspection.

- **Annual accounts:** ensuring their distribution, preparing the directors' report (*see* section 5.7) and filing with the Registrar of Companies within the statutory time period (*see* section 1.2.4).

- **Corporate governance:** advising and reminding directors of their duties and responsibilities, and protecting the company's interests by ensuring that all procedural paperwork is in line with company legislation and that all necessary disclosures are made.

- **Advisers:** acting as a communication channel with non-executive directors (*see* section 2.1) and other advisers.

- **Group structure:** administering any subsidiary companies within the group and maintaining a clear record of group company relationships.

4.12 The future

In March 1998 the DTI issued a consultation document entitled *Modern Company Law for a Competitive Economy.* The document sets out the government's plans for the first major company law review for nearly 40 years. The object of the review is to bring forward proposals for a modern law for a modern world on the basis of the widest possible consultation with all interested parties. After outlining the legislative background, the document goes on to deal with current issues. Broadly, these are complexity, the failure of the law to achieve its purpose, and the relationship between company law and corporate governance.

What are the main points arising from a review of the company law consultation document?

The document outlines the following specific problems of complexity. The document considers that Table A to the Companies Act 1985 is written in technical, legalistic language. There is also excessive detail and in some instances over-regulation.

The document states that an immediate result of this complexity is that companies often have to incur substantial costs in terms of management time and professional fees in taking advice, for example in order to ensure that a particular transaction, which may well be innocent and worthwhile, does not break the rules forbidding companies from giving financial assistance to another person to buy their shares (*see* section 5.3).

The consultation document also highlights examples of the failure of the law to achieve its purpose. One example cited of an ineffective provision of the existing Companies Act is the requirement that companies must keep on their register of members not only the name and address of each member, but also the date on which he or she ceased to be a member (*see* section 5.5.1(c)).

The consultation document also reviews the studies on corporate governance in recent years – Cadbury, Greenbury and Hampel. The document notes that the recommendations of these Committees are currently being combined into a single set of principles and Code of Practice. The document concludes that, in general, the issues raised by these studies are more suitable for best practice than legislation, since the former is more flexible and can be more easily updated. However, the document suggests there may be a need for legislation in certain areas, either because they are not covered by the new Code or experience shows that some legal underpinning is required.

What examples of areas in need of statutory regulation are highlighted by the document?

As has been considered in this book, directors' duties are found in case law rather than in the Companies Act 1985. There is an issue as to whether they should be put into statute, and as to the scope of the duty to act in the company's interest.

In addition, the conduct of annual general meetings is being considered. The DTI has already consulted on changes to the present rules to make it easier for shareholders to table resolutions, and to attend and vote at AGMs if they do not hold shares in their own name. These issues will be considered as part of the review.

Finally, shareholder control over directors' pay is to be reviewed and this will provide an opportunity to examine the responsibilities of shareholders in this and other areas.

What are the terms of reference of the company law review?

The review will consider how core company law can be modernised in order to provide a simple, efficient and cost-effective framework for carrying out business activity which:

- permits the maximum amount of freedom and flexibility to those organising and directing the enterprise;

- at the same time protects, through regulation where necessary, the interests of those involved with the enterprise, including shareholders, creditors and employees; and

- is drafted in clear, concise and unambiguous language which can be readily understood by those involved in business enterprise.

In addition, the review will consider whether company law, partnership law and other legislation which establishes a legal form of business activity together provide an adequate choice of legal vehicle for business at all levels.

When is the final report anticipated?

The final report is intended to be drafted in the autumn of the year 2000 and published in conjunction with a White Paper in March 2001. Any resulting legislation would be for the next Parliament.

Checklist: Duties of directors

1. You owe your duty to the company and to outsiders.

2. You must act in good faith, for proper purposes and with reasonable skill and care.

3. You can be liable for errors of judgement. Do not rely on your co-directors and other officers without question.

4. You must have regard to the interest of your employees.

5. If you are a nominee director you are not a puppet for your appointer.

6. You have a general responsibility to the company's creditors to ensure the company can pay its debts.

7. You cannot make a personal or secret profit.

8. You can have a personal interest in the contract with the company but you must disclose it.

   Are you familiar with the notice procedure?

   Do you know your further disclosure duties in relation to your shareholdings or other interests in the company's securities?

9. Your powers to enter into contracts with the company are extremely limited. You must give full disclosure.

10. You can be sued by the company or by the shareholders in its name if you breach your duties as a director.

11. Are you familiar with the terms or spirit of the Hampel Report?

12. It is a misconception to think that the role of the company secretary is unimportant. In fact its significance is increasing and must be appreciated.

Notes

1 *Re: Neptune (Vehicle Washing Equipment) Ltd* (1995) 1 BCLC 352.

2 *Re: Neptune* Case.

3 *Re: Neptune* Case.

4 *Re: Neptune* Case.

5 Sir Bryan Nicholson, former President CBI.

6 Based upon *Jolley's Company Law Bulletin*, No. 14, March 1998.

5

Your relations with shareholders

5.1 Share transfers

In this chapter the financial structure and membership of the company will be examined.

What is the basic position in relation to share transfers?

Shareholders have a right to transfer their shares and you and your fellow directors must register the transfer. Shares are transferable in the manner provided by the company's articles (*see* section 1.2.3). The articles do not have to place any restriction on transfers of shares but in a private company, in order to ensure that you maintain control over who is admitted to the company, restrictions are usually justified. This is because many private companies are very similar in nature to partnerships.

What are the typical restrictions?

Table A contains restrictions which enable you to refuse to register:

- a transfer of a share which is not fully paid to anybody you do not approve of; and

- a transfer of a share on which the company has a lien. (A lien is the right given to the company to retain possession, or to seek a court declaration for an order for sale of a share which is perhaps unpaid.)

There will generally be a right of *pre-exemption* for existing shareholders to give them the first opportunity to buy any shares which may be for disposal to outsiders.

This means that a shareholder will be permitted to transfer his or her shares to an existing shareholder without restriction. However, where the transfer is to an outsider then a pre-exemption provision will come into effect and you will have no power to register a transfer if you know that the shares have not been transferred first to shareholders and their families. The vendor of the shares will normally give notice to the company secretary who must notify the other shareholders that there are shares available for purchase.

You have no power to authorise registration in circumstances where there would be a breach of the articles.

What are the factors I should consider when exercising my discretion to refuse a transfer?

If you have an absolute discretion to refuse to register there is no limitation on the exercise of your power. Like all other powers you must exercise it bona fide in what you – and not what a court may – consider to be in the interest of the company, and not for any collateral purpose (*see* duty of good faith, section 4.2).

It is for the person alleging any bad faith on your part in coming to your decision to prove it. If the articles do not require you to give any reason for your refusal then do not – silence will not give your challenger anything to point to.

You must fairly consider the matter at a board meeting and pass a resolution to refuse a transfer, and you must give notice of refusal within two months or face a default fine or perhaps a demand for registration by the person you object to.

What can a thwarted shareholder do if I refuse a transfer?

They will have to make application to the court for rectification of the Register. They cannot seek to wind the company up.

The existing shareholder has died or has been declared bankrupt. What can I do?

Whenever a share passes from a deceased or bankrupt shareholder this is known as a 'transmission' rather than a transfer. If a grant of probate (if a will exists) or a grant of administration (if it does not) is produced the company must accept it as evidence of the right of the personal representative or administrator to deal with the shares. However, the company is not bound to accept the representative as a member if it does not approve of him or her. If the articles give you a discretion to refuse registration in any circumstances then this will apply with equal force to the representative.

Can an existing shareholder negate the effect of my refusal to transfer?

Yes, in one instance, although it is unlikely to arise. If the vendor does not promise to secure a registration to the purchaser and you do refuse to register the transfer, the vendor will hold the shares as a trustee for the purchaser.

If a transfer or transmission is sought, how are the shares valued?

This is an extremely important consideration. If the shares are valued too high then any pre-exemption rights may be illusory because existing members simply cannot afford to buy. If they are undervalued the transferor may be aggrieved. Sometimes the articles will fix a price or you may agree the value by negotiation.

It is common for an independent accountant to be appointed to act as valuer who may or may not give reasons to support the valuation. It is notoriously difficult to envisage every circumstance in which shares may have to be valued when articles are drafted, but if the procedure stated in the articles is subsequently followed and it is clearly unfair the transferors cannot easily claim prejudice.

I am the only shareholder as well as the sole director, while my husband or wife will occupy the position of company secretary. Will there be any particular difficulties in the event of my death?

Yes, the single member provisions of the Companies Act do not address this situation. Thus, on your death there will be no shareholder to effect an appointment of a new director (*see* section 2.3), nor will there be any directors to approve the registration of your personal representatives in respect of your shareholdings. Generally, you will have to amend the articles now by empowering them to appoint a new director. That new director can then approve registration of the transmissions to the personal representatives or a transfer from the personal representatives to the beneficiaries.

5.2 Compulsory acquisition of shares

I want to compel a share transfer. What options are available to me?

- If you are a director of a private company the articles may give you a lien or charge on shares for any debts due from the members of the company and give you a power of sale and power to exercise a transfer. However, if you are director of a plc any lien of a public company on its own shares is void unless it is:

  - a lien on partly paid shares for any sums payable in respect of those shares;

  - a lien which is in the ordinary course of business of a lending or credit company;

  - a lien created by the company when it was a private company prior to re-registration as a public company.

- There may be compulsory transfer obligations on a shareholder if he or she is declared bankrupt or is otherwise in breach of the company's regulations.

- You may seek an amendment of the articles where they give a shareholder first refusal in respect of the shares provided such amendment is made in good faith and is not a fraud on the minority (*see* section 5.6.3).

5.3 Financial assistance for acquisition of shares

A private company may now give financial assistance for the purchase of its own shares provided it is solvent and adheres to the statutory procedure set out in the Companies Act 1985 (*see* section 5.7).

5.3.1 The basic position

Section 151(1) provides that if a person is acquiring or proposing to acquire shares in any company it is unlawful for the company or its subsidiary to give financial assistance before or at the same time as the acquisition whether directly or indirectly. Section 151(2) prevents financial assistance for the purpose of subsequently reducing or discharging any liability incurred in purchasing the shares.

What might constitute financial assistance?

A gift, guarantee, security, indemnity, loan or assignment, or other transaction by which the acquirer is directly or indirectly placed in funds.

Any transaction which materially reduces the company's net assets may also amount to financial assistance.

The basic position then is tolerably clear but unfortunately, in common with other restrictions upon corporate self-dealings, the exemptions complicate the position.

5.3.2 The exemptions

The exemptions fall into the following categories:

1 First, where the assistance is given in good faith in the interests of the company; and second, where the assistance for the acquisition or later reduction of the acquirer's liability is not the principal purpose, or it is incidental to some larger purpose. In other words, if it is a genuine commercial transaction which is in the interests of the company.

   This category causes the most difficulty. The courts have stated that 'larger purpose' does not mean 'more important reason' and in the light of the uncertainty surrounding the interpretation of this exception the safer course is to utilise the private company exceptions discussed below.

2 Transactions which are specified as not being prohibited. These include:

   (a) a dividend payment lawfully made may be used to purchase shares in the company;

   (b) a loan made in the ordinary course of business by a money lending company;

   (c) assistance by the company or subsidiary to enable bona fide employees, including you as a director, or their dependants to purchase shares under an employee's share scheme.

However, paragraphs (b) and (c) above only apply to a public limited company if its net assets or distributable profits are not reduced. A loan will not usually reduce net assets as the cash payment will be balanced by a book debt owed to the company.

3 Financial assistance by private companies.

The relaxation of the general prohibition on financial assistance is of great importance to private companies, particularly in terms of facilitating management buy-outs.

Can a company with only one director and shareholder enter into a company purchase of its own shares?

No.

5.4 Insider dealing

This only applies if you are a director of a company listed on the Stock Exchange. As a director you face an array of duties and controls under the law to forbid you from taking advantage of your privileged position within your company. One particular form of profit-making which is greatly criticised is insider dealing. Essentially this involves your use of price-sensitive information known to you but not generally to the public which you have acquired by virtue of your position and you then trade your advantage in the securities in that company. This practice is not limited to directors but can be engaged in by anyone who has access to this type of information.

What should I consider to ensure my actions are not tantamount to insider dealing?

In each case you should carefully consider whether you have inside information which is material to the price of the shares which, if disclosed, would have more than a minimal impact on their selling price. The question you should ask yourself is, would this information affect the decision of a prudent buyer and seller in agreeing to the sale and to the terms? If it would, you must be very careful.

Although the practice is widely criticised, the only statutory restriction is found in the Company Securities (Insider Dealings) Act 1985. This Act, however, makes it a criminal offence only in certain limited circumstances. It does not affect the validity of the action. It is not a blanket prohibition of all insider dealing in securities transactions.

The Responsibilities of Company Directors   Your relations with shareholders

In what situations will the Act apply?

There are three categories of insiders for the purposes of the Act:

- individuals connected with the company;

- individuals contemplating takeover; and

- public servants.

We shall only consider the first two categories in this book.

What does 'connected' with a company mean?

If you are a director of that company or of a subsidiary or its holding company or a subsidiary of its holding company ('a related company'), or you are an employee or other officer of the company or related company, or you occupy a professional or business relationship which exists between (a) your employer or a company of which you are a director, and (b) the first company or a related company.

Give me an example of who may be 'connected persons'.

Executive and non-executive directors (*see* section 2.1), the company secretary, employees, auditors, consultants, solicitors, accountants, bankers and brokers are all within the category.

I am an individual connected with a company. What are the restrictions?

You cannot deal on a recognised stock exchange in securities of a company in certain circumstances. You must now, or at any time in the last six months, have been knowingly connected with the company in question.

I am 'knowingly connected'. Am I therefore in breach?

No, you must also be in possession of unpublished price-sensitive information which you know to be unpublished price-sensitive information in relation to those securities.

What constitutes 'unpublished price-sensitive information'?

This is information which:

- directly or indirectly specifically relates to that company and is not of a general nature relating to that company; and

- is not known to people who are used to dealing in, or would be likely to deal in, those securities but which would, if it were generally known to them, be likely to materially affect the price of those securities. Examples of what information will 'materially affect the price of the securities' might include the announcement of takeover bids, oil or mineral finds, a marked increase or decrease in earnings or the departure of an important executive to a rival company. Also included may be leaks of profit and loss accounts, provisional results and information about share issues.

Whether information is 'unpublished price sensitive information' in a particular instance is always a question of fact for the court to decide but guidance as to what would be specific matters may be obtained from the Model Code for Transactions by Directors of Listed Companies issued by the Stock Exchange. This is to be found in the appendix to Chapter 16 of *The Rules of the Stock Exchange*, known as the Yellow Book, and it imposes restrictions beyond those that are imposed by law.

5.4.1 The Model Code

I am a director in a listed company. Do we need to adhere to the Model Code?

Yes, it is a term of continued listing to introduce and enforce a code relating to the dealings by directors in their own companies' securities which is 'no less exacting' than the Model Code. Therefore, you must have your own dealing code in place, or at least have it on record that the company adopts the Model Code.

What are the major requirements of the Model Code?

1 As a director of a listed company you should not deal, for example buy, sell or exercise an option, in your own company's securities which are traded on the Stock Exchange where you have unpublished price-sensitive information about the company.

2 You must not deal in your company's securities in the two-month period before annual or half-yearly results are announced. There are suitable modifications for companies producing quarterly results.

3 In any event, any dealings must receive clearance from the company chairman or a director appointed to this job. In addition to these 'closed periods', clearance will be refused when the dealing would take place after the need for announcement to the market of unpublished price-sensitive information about the company has become reasonably probable.

4 If you cannot deal, you must stop such dealings by your family and connected persons (see definition of connected persons in section 5.4) with various other institutions, e.g. their investment managers.

5 The board of directors should be kept informed of dealings which have taken place. Each board meeting should have available a list of directors' dealings.

6 Any employees who, while not directors, are likely to possess unpublished price-sensitive information about the company must also comply with the code and it is the duty of you and your fellow directors to ensure that they deal only in accordance with the same.

7 It is important to understand that the Stock Exchange seeks compliance with the spirit and not simply the letter of the code.

What are the consequences if the Model Code is breached?

If you fail to discharge your responsibilities under the Model Code it may lead to censure or worse by the Stock Exchange and possibly suspension or cancellation of listing.

However, a breach of the Model Code is not treated as a presumption of insider dealing.

I am an individual contemplating a takeover. What are the restrictions?

Remember, we are considering two categories of individuals in this book: first, those connected with the company, and second, those contemplating takeovers. Suppose you are contemplating, or have contemplated making, whether with or without another person, a takeover offer for a company in a particular capacity. You cannot deal on a recognised Stock Exchange in securities of that company in another capacity if you have information that the offer is contemplated or you have otherwise unpublished price-sensitive information in relation to those securities.

Remember, 'tippees' (who are persons tipped off by an insider) are also covered by the Act and their actions are similarly outlawed.

Are there any exceptions to what constitutes insider dealing under the Act?

The following should be noted:

- **Acting otherwise than for profit**

  An exception is if you act otherwise than with a view to making a profit or avoiding a loss by the use of the information.

  In addition, you may sell securities if you have to meet a 'pressing financial commitment'. However, this would have to be exceptional.

Another example could be if you are about to retire and are required to exercise your share options immediately or suffer their forfeit.

- **The completion or carrying out of a transaction**

    A further exception is if you are in possession of information relating to a particular transaction and you deal in order to facilitate the completion or carrying out of that transaction. It is not absolutely clear what this exception does and does not legitimise. Imagine the situation where you are buying a large holding in a listed company. If widely known, this fact could well affect the share price, but should not be allowed to paralyse your proposed acquisition. If you then obtain further separate unpublished information which persuades you to expand your purchases to seek a controlling interest, you are presumably not allowed to argue that this is just the continuation or completion of the original transaction.

- **Other categories**

    Certain categories of individuals, for example liquidators, receivers and market-makers, are exempt when they are acting in the ordinary course of business.

5.4.2 Consequences of breach

Is there a power of investigation if insider dealing is suspected?

Yes. If it appears to the Department of Trade and Industry that there are circumstances suggesting that there may have been a breach it may appoint inspectors to investigate suspected insider dealing.

What can the inspectors do?

They can require you to:

- produce for them any documents relating to the company in relation to whose security the contravention is suspected to have occurred or to its securities;

- attend before them to be examined on oath; and

- otherwise give them every assistance which you are reasonably able to give.

You do not have any right to claim privilege against self-incrimination or to be cautioned if you are suspected of an offence.

Are there criminal penalties upon a director for insider dealing?

Yes, you are liable to imprisonment or a fine or both. Any proceedings in England and Wales must be brought by or with the consent of the Department of Trade and Industry or the Director of Public Prosecutions.

5.5 The registers

Name the statutory registers for a private company limited by shares.

- Register of Members

- Register of Charges

- Register of Debenture Holders

- Register of Directors

- Register of Secretaries

- Register of Director Interests

- Minutes of General Meetings

In this book we shall consider the registers of the most practical importance to you as a director.

5.5.1 The Register of Members[1]

Every company must keep a register of its members, that is its shareholders, which gives details of the following:

1 names and addresses of each member;

2 date of registration as a member;

3 date of termination of membership;

4 the numbered shareholding and the class of shares held, for example ordinary, preference, etc.;

5 the amount paid or to be paid on each share.

The date in (2) and (3) above may be of great significance with regard to voting and dividend rights.

What is the purpose of the register?

It provides creditors and investors with information as to the identity of those behind the corporate form which may affect a decision to invest or provide credit.

If yours is a public company the register should be constantly monitored to detect bidders for the company building up a stake with which to launch a takeover bid.

What are the requirements for maintenance of the register?

- It must be kept at the registered office, which is not necessarily your trading address. If the company uses a registrar for the purpose it may be kept at their offices. You must notify the Registrar of Companies of the place where it is kept and whenever its location changes (*see* section 1.2.4).

- You must allow inspection during business hours to any director or shareholder of the company without charge and any member of the public (£2.50 per hour). If a request for a copy of part of the Register is made, copies must be available within ten days. The costs of such copies are:

  - £2.50 for the first 100 entries;

  - £20 for the next 1000;

  - £25 for each subsequent 1000.

  Unfortunately, commercial users can use this information for their own purposes, for example mailing lists. The charge is intended to mitigate this abuse.

- You may close the register up to 30 days per annum by a newspaper advertisement to that effect.

- The register can be rectified by the courts on the grounds of mistake if it is shown that a name has been omitted or not removed or is wrongly entered.

5.5.2 The Register of Substantial Shareholdings

The requirement to keep this register applies only to voting shares in any public company whether or not it is listed.

What is the reason for this register?

It is intended to reveal the accumulation of large shareholdings by stealth or by sudden attacks.

If you have a notifiable interest and it is materially altered or you dispose of such an interest you must notify the company. You must do so where you:

- knowingly acquire a 3 per cent interest by nominal value in the share capital or any class of it; or

- knowingly see your interest fall below that percentage; or

- know that the percentage level of your holding, while remaining above 3 per cent, has nonetheless changed; or

- later become aware of any of these situations.

How do I notify the company?

By written notice specifying the shareholding and any option or conditional purchase arrangements, and the fact that you no longer have a notifiable interest. You must serve the notice within two days of the change and specify that it is served in pursuance of ss 198–202, Companies Act 1985.

I often hear the term 'concert parties' used. What does it mean in the context of change of shareholdings?

A concert party is where apparently independent purchases are in fact made in a coordinated plan to acquire a major shareholding for as low a price as possible and to avoid individually acquiring a notifiable interest. If a concert party exists, each party is treated as having obtained an interest in the others' shareholdings and is under an obligation to disclose them to the company.

What constitutes a 'concert party'?

There must be an agreement to acquire and an actual acquisition of shares involving obligations or restrictions as to their use, retention and disposal.

5.5.3 The Register of Directors and Secretaries

Every company must maintain a Register of Directors and Secretaries.[2] This register, in common with all the other registers, must be kept at the company's registered office and can be inspected by shareholders. The register must state your christian or forename and surname, your nationality, usual residential address, business occupation, date of birth and particulars of any other directorship.

Which other directorships of mine must be shown?

Any directorship, including past directorships, except those you hold with other companies in the same group, or which ceased over five years ago or where your other directorship is with a company which is dormant.

Who else should be made aware of the particulars of my directorship?

The Registrar of Companies (*see* section 1.2.4) within 14 days of any change in your directorship, and within the same period if you are being appointed first director in a newly incorporated business. The Registrar will publish the details in *The London Gazette*, and you should note that until you notify the Registrar and until publishing in the *Gazette* a third party may bind your company to the acts of a director who has in fact retired though this has not yet been notified to the Registrar and published.

What details must be recorded in the register in relation to the company secretary?

The same details as for a director except that the age, occupation and other directorships need not be shown.

What will happen if the registers are not maintained?

Both you and your fellow directors and the company itself are guilty of an offence and a fine of up to £5000 can be imposed. Remember, the current state of the register must be shown in the annual return submitted to the Registrar each year.

It is proposed by the Department of Trade and Industry that your details need not be kept in the Directors Register which is held at the registered office of the company. The information will still be required for filing at Companies House but will not have to be recorded in the Register of Directors.

5.5.4 The Register of Your Share Interests

As a director or a shadow director (*see* section 2.1) you must notify your company of your interest in its shares or debentures. A debenture is a written acknowledgment of indebtedness by a company. Notice must be given within five days of your becoming a director if you already own the shares or within five days of your acquiring or disposing of them. The number, amount, class and price of your shares must be in the notice and your failure to notify will result in a fine or up to two years' imprisonment. There is clear guidance on which 'interest' must be notified in the Companies Act 1985 and space does not permit a review of this topic here. Rather, if in doubt consult your solicitor. Every company must maintain a register of your notices of your share interests, including notices relating to your husband or wife and children. The information must be recorded within three days of receipt, usually by the company secretary (*see* under statutory registers in section 4.11).

Once again this register is open to shareholders free of charge and to the public at a cost of £2.50 per hour. It must be kept at the registered office and be open for inspection throughout the company's annual general meeting (*see* section 7.2.1). Copies can be requested by anyone at a cost of £2.50 for the first 100 entries, £20 for the next 1000 and £15 each subsequent 1000. Failure to maintain the register is punishable by a fine of up to £1000 on each of you as directors and the company.

> *I hold 1000 shares jointly with my husband or wife on trust for our two children. How will my interest be shown in the register?*

> Four separate notices are needed and the register will show a total of 4000 shares, thus the total extent of the interests notified in this instance exceeds the actual number of shares issued.

5.5.5 The Register of Charges and Debentures

Every company must also keep a Register of Charges and Debentures which, while it is your duty as director to ensure they are accurately maintained, do not merit detailed consideration in this report.

> *How long must statutory registers be kept?*

> For the lifetime of the company. However, records of former shareholders and directors can be removed from the register 20 years after the cessation of membership.

5.6 Unfair prejudice

5.6.1 General

It is important that you recognise the distinction between ownership of the company and management of the company. Remember, the shareholders are the owners of the company; the function of management is, as we have seen, usually delegated to the directors (*see* section 3.1). This structure can lead to problems which the courts recognise, and as a director you must be aware that your conduct must not be oppressive or unfair to shareholders. The question usually arises when you and your fellow directors constitute the majority of the members of the company and those shareholders who form the minority complain they are being treated unfairly. Do not make the mistake of thinking that this topic does not affect you. It does and you should be familiar with this aspect of the law.

Give me examples of occasions when minority shareholders may make a complaint?

Perhaps your board considers that the directors should receive the whole of the profits as remuneration, or it may be that you and your fellow directors are using your position to further your private interests instead of those of the company.

What action can shareholders take when they feel they have been prejudiced?

There are five types of action shareholders may bring:

- First, a personal action where some personal individual right has been infringed. This is very rare and hard to substantiate.

- Second, where the same personal right of a number of shareholders has been infringed, a representative action may be brought on behalf of a group of shareholders.

- Third, where a derivative action is brought when the wrongdoers are in control and prevent the company from suing. This is only permitted in exceptional circumstances because the general rule is that the proper complainant in an action in respect of a wrong done to the company is the company. This is known as the Rule in *Foss* v *Harbottle* (*see* section 5.6.2).

- Fourth, aggrieved shareholders may petition the court under s 459, Companies Act 1985 (*see* section 5.6.3).

- Finally, shareholders may petition to have the company wound up on the just and equitable ground under s 122(1)(g), Insolvency Act 1986.

5.6.2 The Rule in *Foss* v *Harbottle*[3]

What is the Rule in Foss v Harbottle?

There are two elements to this so-called Rule. First, as stated, if the complaint is that the wrongdoers are damaging the company it is the company which must bring the action. Second, it is for the majority in most cases to determine whether the company should proceed with an action. Together they form an entirely procedural obstacle to the enforcement of minority shareholders' rights, because it is practically impossible for them to use the company name to bring an action.

Are there any exceptions to the Rule?

Yes, the most important exceptions for present purposes are as follows:

- where your act complained of is illegal, or *ultra vires* (*see* section 3.3);

- where there has been a fraud on the minority and the wrongdoers are in control of the company;

- where s 459, Companies Act 1985, applies (*see* section 5.6.3).

The first exception is self-evident. The second need not involve 'fraud' in its popular connotation, but usually involves misappropriation of company assets or business opportunities (*see* section 4.7).

What actions on the part of a majority will constitute a 'fraud' on the minority?

It is clearly established that the majority cannot appropriate to themselves money, property or advantages which belong to the company or in which the other shareholders are entitled to participate.[4]

Another example of misappropriation is where the majority shareholders willingly compromise litigation commenced by the company on terms advantageous to themselves and usually detrimental to the company and the minority shareholders.

It must be noted that before a shareholder can bring an action for fraud on the minority they must establish that the wrongdoer does in fact have control, i.e. a majority of votes, or that the majority has approved a fraud, or the company is otherwise unwilling to sue. Therefore, some attempt must always be made to persuade the company to sue. Shareholders cannot simply allege that the wrongdoers are in control.

The third exception noted is that provided by s 459, Companies Act 1985.

5.6.3 Section 459, Companies Act 1985

Where the affairs of the company are being or have been conducted in a manner unfairly prejudicial to the interests of its shareholders generally, or to some part of its shareholders, those shareholders can rely on s 459. Section 459 is now used considerably by minority shareholders.

What will the court do to identify the interests of the shareholders alleging prejudice?

The court will look to the individuals within the company and have regard to their rights, expectations and obligations.[5] In addition, all circumstances surrounding their relationship will be considered fully.

One can draw a distinction here between small private companies and larger private and public companies. Small companies may have been formed on the understanding that some or all of the shareholders are to participate in the conduct of the business. In this instance the scope of the legitimate expectations beyond their strict legal rights is much greater because they should expect to receive regular and full information about the conduct of the company's affairs. Conversely, the interests of shareholders in large companies are likely to be very different and much more restricted. Here, shareholders are usually more interested in dividend yield and capital appreciation than involvement in the day-to-day running of the company. If they are dissatisfied they can sell their shares and withdraw from the company. Shareholders in small private companies, however, may not be able to find a ready buyer for their shares. Section 459 applies to all companies, large or small, but the point to appreciate is that it is clearly harder to establish unfairly prejudicial conduct in a larger company.

The courts will look for conduct which, viewed in the light of its effect on the complainant, is 'unfair' and prejudices him or her – it is not necessary to show bad faith.

I am a director and majority shareholder. What actions will constitute 'unfair prejudice'?

An example would be your breach of the Companies Act 1985. This might be your failure to hold general meetings (*see* section 7.2.2), or alternatively the misappropriation of assets or the wrongful exercise of your powers (*see* section 3.3). In addition, s 459 can be used on financial questions, which may include a challenge to your remuneration[6] or the persistent non-payment of dividends, or the payment of very small dividends, perhaps where the dividend has not been increased for many years.[7]

One can see the advantages of adopting the broad structure of the Hampel Report as a private company to avoid the prospect of a shareholder challenge under s 459 on the issue of your remuneration (*see* section 4.10).

Might I be responsible for a single omission only?

Yes. For shareholders to succeed under a s 459 petition they need not show a continuing course of unfair conduct on your part.

What will the court do if unfair prejudice under s 459 is substantiated?

The court may authorise civil proceedings to be brought in the name of the company by any person. This bypasses the Rule in *Foss* v *Harbottle* completely. The court may make an order regulating the future conduct of the company's affairs by altering the memorandum or articles, but if so ordered the company must file the amended documents with the Registrar of Companies as normal. The most common use of s 459 is to procure the buying out of minority shareholders, in other words the court may order the purchase of the petitioners' shares or those of the wrongdoers.

5.6.4 Just and equitable winding-up

An oppressed shareholder may petition the court for a winding-up of the company under s 122(1)(g), Insolvency Act 1986, on the grounds that it is just and equitable to do so. Anyone bringing an action must have shares registered in their name.

What must a shareholder show if they wish to sue under s 122?

They must establish a tangible interest in the winding-up, i.e. there must be a real probability that there will be surplus assets remaining for distribution among the shareholders after the creditors have been paid. Thus, if the company is in fact insolvent, a shareholder cannot petition for a winding-up. If the petition is based on you and your fellow directors' refusal to disclose information to shareholders then the aggrieved shareholders need not establish tangible assets because it is unlikely they will be able to do so.

What are the typical grounds which the court will accept?[8]

The company's basic objective may have failed. Its business may be illegal or fraudulent. Alternatively there might be a deadlock in management or a complete breakdown of confidence. Finally, there may be a breach of obligation contained in the articles or a shareholders' agreement. A shareholders' agreement is an agreement made between the shareholders which is independent of the provisions in the company's articles.

5.7 The directors' report[9]

What is the purpose of the directors' report?

The principal purpose of the report is to review the progress of the company's business.

The directors' report was once a short, formal addition to the accounts but today it is considered to be far more significant.

What should the report contain?

- **Information about you and your fellow directors.** The names of all who have been directors at any time during the financial year must be stated. The extent of your interest in shares or debentures of the company or any holding or subsidiary company must be given. In addition, if during the year the company has paid for insurance to cover you or your fellow directors in respect of possible liability to the company that must also be stated in the report (*see* section 12.2).

- **Information about the company's business.** The report must state the principal activities of the company and any subsidiaries, including any significant change in those activities during the year. It should contain a fair review of the development of the business and its subsidiaries and of their position as at the end of the financial year.

  The report should draw attention to important events affecting the company or any of its subsidiaries since the date of the balance sheet. If the market value of any interests in land held by the company differs substantially from its balance sheet value it should be disclosed if you think the shareholders should be made aware of it.

  The report must include an indication of likely future business developments and of any research and development activities of the company and its subsidiaries.[10] This is important information for shareholders because it represents an application of money which would otherwise generally be available to them. The amount recommended as dividend and the amount proposed to be carried to reserves must also be shown.

- **Information about employment.** Once again, any expenditure on research and development is of interest to your employees as it is likely to play a large part in ensuring the competitiveness of the company and thus its future employment prospects. If your company has over 250 employees the directors' report must now contain a statement describing what action has been taken during the course of the year to promote employee involvement. This includes a statement on consulting employees on matters likely to affect their interests (*see* section 4.4). In addition, if you have over 250 employees, the employment and trading opportunities for disabled employees and health, safety and welfare arrangements for all employees must be detailed.

- **Details of any acquisitions of the company's own shares.** The report must give particulars of any acquisition by the company of its own shares including the total amount paid by the company and the reasons for the purchase (*see* section 5.3).

- **Particulars of any political or charitable donations.** These should also be disclosed in the report.

Is it the directors' responsibility to prepare the report?

The company secretary will prepare the report based on the information which you and your fellow directors provide. The board must approve the report and it must be delivered to the Registrar of Companies (*see* section 1.2.4) signed either by a director or by the company secretary. The name of the signatory must be on every copy of the report.

Do the company's auditors play a part?

Yes, it is common to obtain the auditors' assistance in preparing the report but they must act entirely independently of the board. Considerable weight would be placed on the auditors' interpretation of perhaps vague statements in the report made by you and your fellow directors.

Checklist: Your relations with shareholders

1. Do you know what restrictions your company's articles place upon the transfer of shares by shareholders? Restrictions are not obligatory but to maintain control you should consider certain safeguards, for example pre-emption rights (*see* section 5.1).

2. Are you familiar with what might constitute 'financial assistance' and the exceptions? A private company may give financial assistance for the purchase of its own shares if solvent and the current procedure is followed.

3. Do you understand the concept of insider dealing? Consider whether you are a 'connected' person and possess 'unpublished price-sensitive information'.

4. If you are a director of a public limited company you must know the requirements of the Model Code.

5. Are you aware of your duty to maintain the statutory registers and what those registers are?

6. You must appreciate the exposure you face from aggrieved shareholders who allege unfair prejudice on the part of you or your fellow directors – a single unfair act against a sole shareholder may make you liable.

7. Do you know what information the directors' report should contain?

Notes

1   Based upon Loose, Yelland and Impey (1995).

2   Section 288, Companies Act 1985.

3   *Foss* v *Harbottle* (1843) 67 ER 189.

4   *Burland* v *Earle* (1902) ACH 3.

5   *Re: Postgate and Denby (Agencies) Ltd* (1987) BCLC 8.

6   *Re: A Company (No. 002162 of 1984)* (1985) BCLCAT.

7   *Re: Sam Weller Ltd* (1990) CH 682. *See also* Farrah, Furey and Hannigan (1991).

8   EC Council Directive 78/660, Art 46.2(B)(C).

9   Based on Farrah, Furey and Hannigan (1991).

10 EC Council Directive 78/660, Art 46.2(B)(C).

6

Relations of directors with one another: fate chooses your relations – you choose your fellow directors

In any company the people are important – so too are the relations between them. While it is not expected that you will agree with all your fellow directors all the time – indeed such a state of affairs is unlikely to be found in a healthy board – there must be some general agreement of approach between all the directors. Questions of your relations with your other directors do not normally arise unless there is disagreement or default.

6.1 Disagreement with fellow directors

What happens when the inevitable disagreements occur?

The articles usually provide that questions at board meetings be decided by a majority vote, each director having one vote. Therefore, disagreements are generally resolved by a counting of heads.

An important guide is to avoid becoming a 'yes' man to a dominant chairman or managing director. The risk of liability for breach of duty is just as acute if you do not play your proper part. As a director you are expected to apply your own judgment to company matters.

I find myself in disagreement with the policy of my fellow directors. What should I do?

Your first course of action should be to raise the matter at a board meeting. If there is none scheduled, check the company's articles to establish whether you have the right to convene a meeting (see section 7.1.1). In most instances you will have this ability but there is of course no guarantee that your fellow directors will attend. The issue will then have to be voted upon at board level.

I have been outvoted at the board meeting but do not wish the matter to rest there. What should I do next?

Being overruled by your colleagues is something one has to accept from time to time in commerce. If you attach great importance to the matter you may insist that your dissent be minuted but nonetheless accept that in deferring to the majority decision you are doubtless acting in the best interest of the company.

You may feel that you have no alternative – and, indeed, in some cases a duty – to refuse to accept the decision of your fellow directors. This may be either because the intended course of the board is likely to be extremely detrimental to the company or, worse still, illegal.

As explained earlier, your duty as a director is not to give passive consent to every decision and you will not be discharging your duties fully if you merely vote against the issue and no more. It may be prudent to insist that the company's legal advisers be brought in to consider the position.

Can I bring the matter to a general meeting?

Yes. If you control or can count upon the support of a substantial part of the voting power this may be very effective. It is essential that you remember that a decision in general meeting cannot bind the board but clearly directors cannot continue for very long pursuing a policy against the wishes of the shareholders.

The general meeting may be the annual general meeting but if you cannot meet until then you may call an extraordinary general meeting if you control or can obtain the support of 10 per cent of the paid-up shares (*see* section 7.2.2(a) for procedure to call a general meeting).

If I call a general meeting, what might the resolution be?

The following are perhaps obvious resolutions:

1   That the meeting has no confidence in the policy adopted by the board.

2   That a shareholders' committee be appointed to investigate the question. Consideration should be given to the appointment of an independent chairman of that committee.

3   That the directors be removed from office and others be appointed in their place.

4   That a Department of Trade and Industry inspector be appointed.

Remember, you must give proper notice of any resolution, and if you seek the removal of any director, 'special notice' is required (*see* section 7.2.2(b)).

6.2 Resignation

Should I stay or should I go? I am unable to refer the matter to a general meeting or I have done so and failed to obtain support. What next?

It may be that your only option is to resign from the board. You may wish to publish a statement for the benefit of shareholders setting out the reasons for your decision. Do not take the decision to resign easily. You must act in the best interest of the company (*see* section 4.2) and it could be that your departure will cause more harm than if you attempt to improve the position by staying.

My fellow directors wish me to resign. What should I consider?

One can resign from the office of director at any time, subject to the terms of any relevant provision in your service contract (*see* section 10.1). However, there might be publicity considerations which mean that it would be preferable for you to resign rather than be removed. Once again your paramount consideration is what is in the interest of the company and if this leads you to resolve to stay and fight, so be it. Remember, if your fellow directors intend to pass a resolution in general meeting for your removal you are entitled to circulate a statement to shareholders setting out your side of the matter (*see* section 10.2).

6.3 Department of Trade and Industry investigation

Can I call in Department of Trade and Industry inspectors?

Yes, but only where you consider there have been serious irregularities on the part of your fellow directors.

The DTI inspectors can investigate the company's affairs together with ownership, control and material influence over the company.

As a director, you cannot alone involve the DTI. It will be necessary for you to obtain sufficient support from other shareholders. To invoke an investigation, application must be made by either:

- not less than 200 members; or

- members holding not less than 10 per cent of the issued shares; or

- 20 per cent of the members if there is no share capital; or

- a majority decision of the board of directors.

What information will the DTI need?

You must furnish sufficient information as the DTI requires to show that you and your fellow applicants have good reason to involve the inspectors. The DTI may ask you jointly to put up not more than £5000 as security for the cost of the investigation.

Your name and those of the other applicants will not be disclosed to the directors whom you seek to censure but they will be given the chance to meet the case against them.

It is important to realise that the power of the DTI to appoint inspectors to investigate the affairs of the company may also be invoked by the courts or by the DTI itself. This will be the case if it appears that the company's business has been conducted in a fraudulent, unlawful or unfairly prejudicial manner to some of its members, or alternatively that its members have not been given all the information with respect to the company's affairs which they might reasonably expect.

The power of the DTI should be a forceful deterrent to malpractice. The publicity the appointment of inspectors will attract will be disastrous and it must be assumed that the report will be published.

Aside from compiling a report on the company, can the DTI take further action?

Yes, it can apply to the courts for an order to disqualify recalcitrant directors or to protect the interest of the minority shareholders. It can, in extreme cases, apply to the courts to have the company wound up. In any proceedings the DTI report can be used in evidence to support the inspectors' opinions and the facts found by the inspectors when a disqualification order is sought (*see* section11.3.7).

There is a third step: the inspectors can compel directors and others to produce documents and answer questions on oath if necessary. Refusal can lead to proceedings for contempt of court. Moreover, any answer which contains any admission may be used as evidence against that individual, even in a criminal trial.

If in the course of its investigation the DTI believes there is something seriously amiss it can suspend its enquiry and call in the Serious Fraud Office (SFO). However, the SFO have to operate within the ambit of the Police and Criminal Evidence Act 1984 which gives several rights to a suspect. The DTI, by contrast, need give no caution, there is no privilege against self-incrimination, and they need not warn the director until a very advanced stage that he or she is not merely a witness but a suspect.

6.4 Winding-up

I feel the only solution to the matter is to put the company into liquidation. Can I do so?

Yes, but only if a 75 per cent majority of the shareholders can be secured to pass a special resolution. The liquidation can be carried out as a voluntary winding-up, and if a declaration of solvency can be made, it can be a members' voluntary winding-up and be under the control of the shareholders.

It can be seen that the winding-up option is in practice confined to private companies akin in characteristics to partnerships.

6.5 Court application

I cannot obtain a 75 per cent majority to pass the resolution. Can I apply to the courts?

Yes. The basis for such an application is that it is 'just and equitable' to wind the company up (*see* section 5.6.4). The courts have held the following to be satisfactory:

- The main objective of the company has failed.

- The business is fraudulent, non-existent or illegal.

- There has been persistent oppression, for example where the directors have persistently refused to supply accounts or information.

- The company is a quasi-partnership and the directors have become 'deadlocked' or are unable to continue the management.

- One party who is entitled to participate in the directorship or management has been excluded.

Checklist: Your relations with your fellow directors

1. Do not simply be a 'yes' man to a dominant chairman or managing director.

2. You should know the options open to you if you disagree with your fellow directors – raise the issue at a board meeting, have your dissent minuted, take the matter to a shareholders' general meeting, consider resignation. Should the DTI be contacted or the company wound up?

7

Proceedings of directors

board. If you or any other director are interested in a transaction which is to be discussed (*see* section 4.8), and you or they are not permitted by the articles to vote or count in the quorum on that particular item of business, you, or the relevant director, are not counted for the purposes of the quorum.

What happens if the meeting is inquorate?

Your meeting is irregular and cannot transact business. However, once again, there is nothing to prevent a subsequent meeting with an effective quorum ratifying an invalid resolution and outsiders will not be prejudiced.

7.1.3 Resolutions of directors

At your board meeting you will exercise your powers by resolutions which are passed in the manner laid down in the articles or agreed upon by each of you under powers granted by the articles. As stated, resolutions are usually passed by a majority of votes of those present. It is generally acceptable to admit proxies and for the chairman to be given a casting vote.

Does the decided issue have to be embodied in a formal resolution?

No, although it is clearly better management to do so. The minutes recording the decision need only enter the substance.

Can a particular subject or issue always be determined by only one board meeting?

Not necessarily. In order to carry a resolution into effect, it is sometimes a requirement to do some further act in the name of the company. For example, you may resolve to borrow money. It will be necessary to apply to a lender or to issue a prospectus, and when the lender is found or the security agreed on, you will need to pass another resolution approving the terms and directing that the contract be executed. Thus, a matter may come before the board several times before it is completed.

I and my fellow directors are frequently very busy. Do we always have to meet to discuss a matter to be decided?

No, it is sometimes impracticable for all of you to assemble to consider a particular matter. The company's articles will usually allow you to use written resolutions signed by all the directors entitled to receive notice of a board meeting. Any decision so taken will be as effective as if passed at a board meeting (*see* section 7.2.2(g)).

7.1.4 Minutes

Following your meeting, it is the duty of the company's secretary to record the decisions taken in the form of minutes.

Every company must ensure that minutes of all proceedings of general meetings and board meetings be entered in books kept for that purpose. This is a requirement of statute but will also usually be a requirement of your articles.

If yours is a large company, it is common for copies of draft minutes to be circulated following approval by the chairman to those of you who are directors concerned with the particular subject matter for possible amendment before the minutes are agreed and recorded in the Minute Book.

What are the penalties for failure to maintain minutes?

The company and every officer in it is liable to a fine of up to £1000 and up to £100 for each day the default continues.

Why is it so important to keep minutes?

Aside from the legal necessity, it is good management to maintain minutes. It may prove necessary for the company to prove that a particular decision was taken or that the proper procedure was observed in relation to some action. Failure to keep accurate minutes may prove to be a costly omission as, although unrecorded business may be proved by other evidence, signed minutes or records constitute the best evidence if duly signed by you or any other director or the company secretary (*see*, for example, section 3.6).

Are signed minutes conclusive evidence of the business transacted?

No, unless stated as such in the articles, they are only 'evidence' of what was done in the absence of any evidence to the contrary. For example, the testimony of someone present at the meeting can be admitted by the courts to show that the minutes or records are incomplete or inaccurate.

Who should sign the minutes?

Usually the chairman but if you have no chairman the minutes may be signed by an officer of the company. However, in this instance you should ensure that the board not only approve the minutes as a correct record but also resolve to specifically authorise the officer concerned to sign the minutes. Failure to so authorise leaves the company and the validity of the minutes open to attack by anyone seeking to challenge the same and will undoubtedly be seized upon by lawyers representing that party.

I and my fellow directors agree that the minutes are a true record of a particular decision but consider that the decision should not have been taken. What should we do?

You should leave the minutes as a true record of what was done but pass a new resolution at a properly constituted board meeting rescinding the decision.

I and my fellow directors have decided that the minutes do not accurately record what happened. What must we do?

The necessary corrections should be made and initialled by the chairman when he signs the minutes. However, no alteration should ever be made after the minutes have been signed.

I was present at the meeting which approved the minutes of a previous meeting from which I was absent. Am I responsible for decisions recorded in the minutes of the first meeting?

No. However, you should be careful when approving the first minutes to avoid the use of the word 'confirm' which might suggest that you participated in the decision.

What should the content of the minutes consist of?

Minutes are not a report of the meeting, merely a record of decisions taken. It is usual to include a short narrative to lead up to the decision.

I voted against the decision taken but was in the minority. Should that be recorded?

Not unless you feel very strongly that the wrong decision has been taken. In that instance you should ask that your objections be recorded in the minutes.

Who is entitled to see minutes of the board of directors?

Any director of the company, and also the auditors of the company are entitled to have access to the minutes. Shareholders, however, have no right to inspect or have copies of board minutes and they should therefore be kept entirely separate from minutes of general meetings of shareholders.

Remember, while irksome, it is extremely important that full minutes be kept of every board meeting. It will only be a matter of time before you pay for your failure so to do.

7.1.5 General procedure

As explained, it is up to you and your fellow directors to regulate your own procedure, but the following is a precis of what should usually be done:

1 While not compulsory, it is useful to keep an attendance book and sign the attendance of each director as appropriate.

2 You should circulate an agenda before the meeting together with copies of minutes of the last meeting and any document or perhaps the accounts which may require study beforehand.

3 You should decide by a majority vote on a show of hands. Unless the articles give you weighted voting rights the size of your shareholding is irrelevant when voting.

4 You can dispense with a meeting altogether if written resolutions are signed by all the directors. This is normally authorised by the articles.

Do we need to file a Form 288 on the appointment or change of the company secretary?

Yes, Form 288 is the form used when appointing a director or secretary and is available from any law stationers.

Is it necessary to file a Form 288 in respect of the appointment of an assistant company secretary?

No, not in order to notify Companies House of the appointment of an assistant secretary. However, it would be necessary in respect of the appointment of a joint secretary.

7.2 The general meeting

The general meeting or 'shareholders' meeting' is the formal occasion at which business given to the shareholders by the company's articles or by law is conducted. The nature of these meetings varies from the media showpiece of the large public company to the informal gathering of the small family business. By and large the rules governing both are the same.[2]

My company has an audio-visual link with its other offices. Can we still hold a shareholders' meeting?

Yes, provided all the shareholders can participate fully in the meeting. However, the question whether a valid meeting can be held where no one is able to meet face to face but only via audio-visual link remains unanswered.[3]

There are two types of general meeting: the annual general meeting (AGM) and the extraordinary general meeting (EGM).

7.2.1 The annual general meeting

Every company must hold an AGM in each calendar year and these must not be more than 15 months apart.

I have just incorporated my company and started trading with my fellow shareholders. When need we call the first AGM?

You need not call your first AGM in the first or second calendar year of incorporation provided you hold it within 18 months of incorporation.

The AGM must be specified as such in the notice or otherwise it will not be considered as such for the purpose of the obligation to hold one in each year.

What happens if the company fails to hold an AGM?

Every officer, which includes all directors and *de facto* directors, will be liable to a fine of up to £5000. However, a private company may choose to dispense with the need to hold an AGM by passing what is known as an 'elective' resolution. If so passed no AGM need be held in the year the resolution is passed, nor indeed in any subsequent year the resolution is passed.

What are the usual topics for discussion at the AGM?

Your company's articles may specifically state what should be considered at the AGM but if they do not then the following are normally considered:

* the accounts and balance sheet;

* the directors' and auditors' reports;

* any declaration of dividends;

* the election of directors;

* the appointment and remuneration of auditors;

* any other business.

Unfortunately the accounts are not ready for the forthcoming AGM. What should we do?

You must proceed with the AGM in any event and deal with the laying of the accounts and reappointment of the auditors at a later date. Alternatively, if yours is a private company, you may dispense with the requirement to lay accounts or reappoint auditors annually by once again passing an elective resolution.

If your company is listed on the Stock Exchange then all directors' service contracts or details thereof must be made available for inspection at the registered office by anyone from the date of the notice convening the meeting until the meeting is closed.

7.2.2 The extraordinary general meeting

Any other general meeting is an EGM and you and your fellow directors may call one whenever you think fit. As with your other powers, you must act in good faith and not select a time and a place for the meeting with the intention of making it difficult for certain shareholders to attend (*see* section 5.6.3).

Can I and my co-directors be compelled to call an EGM?

Yes, if the shareholders who hold at least 10 per cent of voting shares (if fully paid for) call for one. Those shareholders must state the purpose of the meeting, and sign and deposit their requisition at the registered office. Remember, your registered office may not be your trading address!

What if the directors refuse to call the meeting even though requested as above by the appropriate shareholders?

After 21 days following their request the shareholders who called for the meeting, or alternatively those who hold more than half of their voting rights, may, no more than 28 days after the original request, call a meeting within three months of that date. Their expenses for calling and attending the meeting will be deducted from your remuneration and that of any other defaulting director.

Who else may call a meeting?

At least two shareholders provided they hold 10 per cent of the issued share capital (regardless of their voting right) unless the company's articles state otherwise. You must therefore check your articles. A resigning auditor may call a meeting if they consider there are circumstances surrounding their resignation which need to be brought to the attention of shareholders or creditors. Their notice of resignation to the directors must also include a statement of the circumstances for discussion.

Who normally sends out the notices of the EGM on behalf of the directors?

The company secretary, but you must ensure that he or she has been given authority by the board to do so. If, however, no authority is given before sending the notices the board can subsequently ratify the distribution of the notices.

(a) Notice of general meeting

To whom must notice be given?

Every shareholder of the company unless the articles state otherwise. Anyone who does not have a registered address in the UK is not entitled to notice.

What is the effect of failure to give notice to everyone entitled to it?

The meeting is invalid. Therefore you should ensure that your company's articles allow for 'accidental omission' in giving notice without rendering the proceedings invalid. If the articles do not contain this proviso, take steps to change the articles.

How should notice be given?

It should always be in writing but other than that requirement it depends upon the company's articles. For example, you may wish to change your articles to enable a newspaper advertisement to constitute notice rather than an individual mailing to shareholders. Usually the articles require notice to be sent by post, and if properly addressed and stamped it is deemed to be given 48 hours after posting.[4] If your articles state deemed notice by post in 24 hours, change the articles if you intend sending notices by second-class post.

If yours is a public company with its shares listed on the Stock Exchange, notice must appear in at least one national newspaper and the advertisement must be sent in advance to the Stock Exchange for approval.

What is the length of notice required for general meetings?

An AGM requires at least 21 days' written notice and an EGM at least 14 days' written notice unless a special resolution or elective resolution is to be proposed in which case 21 days is required. For an explanation of special and elective resolutions *see* subsection (e) below.

These periods must be clear days' notice and so do not include the day of sending or the day of the meeting. For example, the EGM is scheduled for 24 November. The last date for sending the notice is therefore 1 November. However, you must be careful. If postal notice is deemed to be 48 hours after postage then 31 October would be your last day for sending notice.

Can shorter notice be agreed and what percentage of shareholders must sign a consent to short notice to an AGM or EGM?

Yes. If you wish to call an AGM, all shareholders entitled to attend and vote must agree to short notice. However, if you wish to call an EGM then the majority of shareholders if they hold 95 per cent in value can agree short notice.

This ability is very useful for a private company with few shareholders and if yours is such a company you can dispense with notice altogether provided all shareholders agree to pass a resolution so dispensing. This cannot be done if an elective resolution is to be passed at the meeting and 21 days is required.

What should be included in the notice?

Careful thought must be given to this question as all business transactions at an EGM must be specified in the notice convening the meeting. Certainly the place, time and general nature of the business must be specified. In addition the notice must clearly state the right of every shareholder to appoint a proxy who need not be a shareholder.

(b) Special notice

There are certain ordinary resolutions which require a mere majority of shareholders to be carried which require what is known as special notice, i.e. 28 days. These are:

- to remove a director;
- to appoint a director aged 70 or over to a public company;
- to appoint a new auditor, remove an auditor before the expiration of his or her term of office or fill a casual vacancy in the office of auditor.

How is special notice given?

The intending proposer must give the company at least 28 days' notice before the meeting. The company must then give notice of the resolution to the shareholders not less than 21 days before the meeting.

What if my co-directors and I call the general meeting less than 28 days after the special notice is served on us?

The notice which you give is still valid.

Can we, as directors, give notice to the shareholders by newspaper advertisement?

Yes, if that newspaper has appropriate circulation or by any other method allowed by the company's articles, but in any event at least 21 days before the meeting.

(c) Quorum for general meeting

What is the minimum number of shareholders who must be present to allow the legal transaction of business?

At least two shareholders must be present in person, unless your articles state otherwise. The quorum must be present at the beginning and throughout the meeting.

I am also a shareholder in the company and hold shares in two capacities, one as a trustee under a trust and also in my private capacity.

In this instance you can count as two members for the purpose of the quorum.

What happens if the quorum is not present at the beginning or is lost during the general meeting?

The company's articles will usually require the meeting to be adjourned for one week and the subsequent meeting must attain the same quorum as laid down in the articles. You and your fellow directors may decide this period of adjournment in your discretion by amending the articles if necessary.

(d) The chairman

Any director may act as chairman of a general meeting. Usually the chairman of the board will act but if unwilling or unable then you and your co-directors can appoint one of your members. If you are appointed chairman you must conduct the meeting properly and maintain order. It is you who will decide the length of address of any shareholder but you must give shareholders a reasonable opportunity to speak. Generally, your company's articles will give you a casting vote in the event of a tie.[5]

When must a chairman be appointed?

It is always entirely optional.

(e) Resolutions

There are four types of resolution.

- **Ordinary resolutions**

  This is the usual form in which decisions are taken by the general meeting and the other three types of resolutions are very much the exception. An ordinary resolution will be passed if a simple majority of those voting (not necessarily present) vote in favour of it.

- **Extraordinary resolutions**

  Here, 75 per cent of those voting must vote in favour of the resolution. The main instance where an extraordinary resolution is needed is where the company wishes to be wound up because it cannot meet its liabilities. It is important that you do not confuse an extraordinary resolution with an extraordinary general meeting. An extraordinary resolution can be passed at an EGM or/and an AGM.

- **Special resolutions**

  Of those voting, 75 per cent must vote in favour of the resolution but the notice calling the meeting must be given at least 21 days in advance and state clearly that the resolution is a special resolution. However, if 95 per cent of the shareholders entitled to attend and vote agree, less than 21 days' notice can be given and a valid special resolution still passed. The usual occasion when a special resolution is required is where a major constitutional change is involved, for example where the shareholders wish to change the articles or objects of the company or reduce its share capital. The memorandum of the company is a statement setting out what the company is empowered to do in its relationship to the outside world. The 'object' of the company is a clause contained in the memorandum and simply states the nature of the business which the company carries on (*see* section 1.2.2).

- **Elective resolutions**

  Elective resolutions were introduced in an attempt to 'deregulate' the running of private companies. In fact they do not entirely succeed. There must be a unanimous agreement of all shareholders who are entitled to attend and vote.

  Is it possible to call a meeting at short notice to pass an elective resolution?

  Yes, it is now possible under the provisions of s 379A of the Companies Act 1985. However, an elective resolution must be approved by 100 per cent of the membership of the company holding voting rights.

  The occasions requiring an elective resolution are elections:

  - to dispense with the laying of accounts and reports before a general meeting;

  - to dispense with holding an AGM;

  - to decide the majority required to authorise short notice of meeting;

  - to dispense with the appointment of auditors annually;

  - to decide the duration of a director's power to allot shares in the company (the articles will give you a power to distribute shares to shareholders but this is generally limited for a specified period).

It can be seen that a meeting called to pass an elective resolution cannot be held on short notice.

(f) Registration of resolutions

Sometimes the resolutions which you and your fellow directors, or the shareholders, of the company pass are of concern to third parties. In these cases the law requires you to register the resolutions with the Registrar of Companies.

When must I register such resolutions?

Within 15 days of their passing.

Which resolutions require registration?

The following are the most common examples:

- all special resolutions;

- all extraordinary resolutions;

- all elective resolutions;

- resolutions agreed to by all shareholders but which would otherwise be invalid unless passed as special or extraordinary resolutions;

- a resolution for the voluntary winding-up of the company.

If the company has passed a special resolution to amend the articles or memorandum then the amended articles or memorandum must also be registered together with the resolution to amend.

(g) Written resolutions

If yours is a private company, anything which may be done by ordinary, special, extraordinary or elective resolution may be achieved by a written resolution, apart from a resolution to remove a director or auditor. Written resolutions are an alternative to resolutions passed at a meeting and thus avoid the need to call a formal meeting. In addition, no notice need be given to pass a written resolution.

How do we pass a written resolution?

All shareholders entitled to attend and vote at the meeting must sign the written resolution or sign on behalf of a shareholder who has given consent. The resolution is passed when the last member signs the written resolution.

Do all signatures have to be on the same document?

No, provided each signature is written on a document which accurately states the terms of the resolution.

A copy of the resolution must be sent to the company's auditors. If, within seven days, the auditors inform you that the resolution must be passed at a general meeting the resolution passed in writing will be ineffective unless so passed at a meeting. In addition, unless the auditors otherwise confirm that the resolution does not concern them as auditors or need not be considered in a general meeting, the written resolution will have no effect.

(h) Proxies

As a director you should be familiar with the proxy procedure.

What is meant by the term 'proxy'?

'Proxy' refers to both the agent appointed by a shareholder to vote on his or her behalf at a meeting of the company and to the actual document appointing that agent.

Is there any value in adopting the proxy machinery to the board?

Yes, if shareholders are to vote at all they are far more likely to do so via the proxy voting mechanism than to attend in person at the meeting and vote there. In addition, if you honestly believe it to be in the best interests of the company, you may use the company's money to pay for the cost of sending out and returning proxy forms, even if they only invite shareholders to appoint one of your board to vote in favour of the board's policy. However, in this instance you must send out proxies to every shareholder entitled to notice and to vote by proxy at the meeting.

What right does a proxy have?

He or she has the right to attend all meetings but may only vote on a show of hands if permitted by the articles. For example, Table A (*see* section 1.2.3) does not permit proxies to vote on a show of hands. Therefore you must check your articles.

A proxy may, however, always vote on a poll and in a private company a proxy has the same right to speak as the shareholder or director appointing him or her. However, in a public company the right to speak will depend on the articles.

Where will I find the form of the document appointing a proxy for guidance?

In your articles. If there are minor variations to this suggested form, this will not invalidate the proxy.

It should be noted that a proxy appointment is conditional on the director or shareholder themselves not attending the meeting and if he or she does so the proxy is ineffective.

What happens if the proxy is terminated?

One can terminate a proxy at any time. However, it may be that a proxy has been ended without the knowledge of the company or other shareholders. Usually the articles will state that a vote passed by a proxy shall be valid unless the company has been notified in writing before the meeting. This does not alter the position between the proxy and his or her appointer, but it does protect the company if it treats as valid a vote cast by a proxy's authority, which unknown to the company has ended.

The notice of meeting (*see* sections 7.1.1 and 7.2.2(a)) must state the right to appoint the proxy and the validity of proxies is decided by the chairman whose decision is final.

Can a company which is registered in England and Wales and which has foreign directors and shareholders hold its annual or extraordinary general meetings overseas?

Yes. This is a fairly common practice. Case law on this subject merely indicates that the venue should be in a convenient place for shareholders.

Checklist: Directors' proceedings

1. You will be involved with two kinds of meetings: board and general meetings.

2. Do you know how to convene a board meeting in your company? Check the quorum.

3. You must always keep minutes of your board meetings.

4. Check that you understand the general procedure for board meetings.

5. What are the typical topics for discussion at the AGM?

6. Are you familiar with the procedure for calling an AGM and for passing resolutions? Ensure that you understand the various types of resolutions, i.e. ordinary, extraordinary, special, elective and written.

7. Do you appreciate the value and rights of a proxy?

Notes

1 Based on Loose, Yelland and Impey (1995).

2 Based on Farrah, Furey and Hannigan (1991).

3 *Byng* v *London Life Association Ltd* (1989).

4 Article 115, Table A.

5 Article 50, Table A.

8

Directors' remuneration – management and money go hand in hand

It is important to know that the mere fact you hold office as a director does not in itself entitle you to remuneration. This is a matter for the articles. Authority is usually found in the articles by virtue of Art 82, Table A, which provides that your remuneration shall from time to time be determined by the company in general meetings. Alternatively, the power may be delegated to the board and Art 84 provides that the board may determine the remuneration of the managing and executive directors.

If you are a director in a large public company, the task is frequently delegated to a remuneration committee, composed mainly of non-executive directors. You must be able to show authority for your remuneration, otherwise it is liable to be reclaimed by the company or by a liquidator.

The amount of remuneration you receive is a matter of internal management and it is not subject to a requirement of reasonableness unless it is in truth a disguised gift and it is paid out of capital. However, you should bear in mind the recommendations of the Hampel Report (*see* section 4.10).

8.1 Expenses

Can I claim travelling expenses?

Yes, authority for your claiming travelling, hotel and other expenses is found in the articles. If you have a service contract with the company the terms of that contract will usually amplify and specify those rights (*see* section 9.3.9). This right is of great practical benefit to you because you are entitled to deduct expenses 'wholly, exclusively and necessarily' incurred in the performance of your duties from your income for the purposes of assessment to income tax. The onus is, however, upon you to justify any deductions.

8.2 Your tax treatment

Can I be paid free of income tax?

No, any provision for payment of remuneration free of income tax will be treated as if it is provided for payment as a gross sum subject to income tax. You must ensure that all remuneration paid by the company is net of income tax.

How will I be taxed?

Your liability to tax falls under Schedule E and PAYE applies just as it does for employees. The company as your employer must calculate and deduct all appropriate tax from payments made to you and must retain documents and records relating to the calculation of PAYE for at least three years. These deductions to PAYE apply whether you are subject to basic or higher rate income tax.

I am late in sending in on behalf of the company the monthly remittance to the Inland Revenue. What are the consequences?

The Inland Revenue can estimate the amount of tax and National Insurance due. You will then have seven days in which to send a return showing the correct amount and pay that sum. Otherwise the estimated sum must be paid even if it is much greater than the actual liability. Any sum overpaid as a result of this process may be deducted from subsequent payments or repaid at the end of the tax year.

I am to receive compensation for loss of office. Is there any charge to tax?

Generally yes unless the compensation is paid:

- on your loss of office as a result of death or disability;

- in certain cases where your employment has included foreign service; and

- for a sum under £30 000, provided it is made 'in connection with' termination of employment.

Do I need to be mindful of the company's liability to corporation tax?

Yes, you must on behalf of the company make returns to the Inland Revenue of its profits for each accounting period. If a return is not made, you still have an overriding obligation to notify the company's liability to tax.

Assessments can be raised by the Revenue at any time up to six years after the end of the period concerned, and so you must keep records for at least that length of time.

If you have been guilty of fraudulent or negligent conduct, assessments can be raised up to 20 years after the end of the chargeable period to which the assessment relates. The Revenue has wide powers to investigate the company's tax affairs and can require the company and you to produce any documentation relevant to the company's tax liabilities.

8.2.1 VAT

Under the VAT Act, you – on behalf of the company – must register with the authorities and keep relevant records and accounts for up to six years.

8.2.2 National Insurance

Liability for National Insurance is an extremely complex area and you must obtain professional advice, but you may note the following:

- You will be treated as a Class 1 contributor if you receive remuneration.

- Earnings-related contributions will be collected under the PAYE procedure together with liability to income tax.

- If you have more than one directorship or source of earnings you should generally make contributions on your total earnings.

The company's liability to pay employees' contributions can be enforced by the Department of Social Security in criminal proceedings and in defence of any prosecution the company must show that the contributions were not in fact payable. You, as director, will be liable to pay such contributions personally if you know, or ought reasonably to have known, of the company's failure to pay. Your liability will not cease upon your retirement from the company.

8.3 Share incentive schemes – a share of the action

You may be rewarded by having the option to acquire shares at a favourable price. This may be either:

- having a genuine option to acquire;

- issuing shares to you of which a very small element of the capital is paid up; or

- providing you with a loan facility.

This arrangement is known as a share incentive scheme and is quite lawful. You will be taxed upon any benefits you receive from the scheme unless you fall within certain exemptions which include approved profit-sharing schemes, registered profit-related pay schemes and executive share option schemes. The tax treatment of each of these exceptions is ever changing and consideration of such tax will not be given in this book. The company's auditors should be consulted upon the benefits of the various schemes.

Is my remuneration shown in the accounts?

Yes, the company's accounts must show all sums paid to you by way of remuneration, including all expenses which are chargeable to income tax.

What details will be disclosed?

The total pensions contribution paid to you and the total compensation paid to you for loss of office including any sums paid on your retirement.

It is your duty to notify the company in writing of your emoluments to enable the company to show the requisite information in the accounts. You must disclose facts which are unknown to the company, such as payments from other parties and expenses which have been charged to income tax.

8.4 Loans to directors

'To every rule there is an exception' is a statement which sums up the law governing loans to directors.

The start point in the review of your ability to take a loan is the 'no conflict' rule. You must not place yourself in a position where your duties and your personal interests conflict. You must always bear in mind your overriding duty to act in the best interest of the company and the law reinforces these rules by extensive prohibitions against loans to you and your family. Even where transactions are permitted by the Companies Act, more restrictive provisions may exist in the company's articles and memorandum.

The law in relation to this topic is considerably complex and professional advice must be obtained by the company before any of the transactions set out below are entered into.

8.4.1 The general rule

What is the general rule?

1 No company can make a loan, or provide a guarantee or other security to you for a loan made to you by a third party.

2 No plc can make a quasi-loan to you or to a person 'connected' with you or give any form of security for loans or quasi-loans made by a third party to you or a connected person.

What is a quasi-loan?

This is where the company pays money on behalf of either you or a connected person, or reimburses a third party for expenditure incurred on your behalf and for which you are obliged to repay that third party. An example is the provision of a credit card for your use on the basis that the company will pay the bill initially and you will reimburse the company later.

Who is a connected person?

A connected person is either:

1 your husband or wife, child or stepchild; or

2 a company in which you and, if relevant, your husband, wife, child or stepchild are interested in at least 20 per cent of the equity share capital or can exercise or control more than 20 per cent of the voting power at any general meeting; or

3 a trustee of any trust if you or anybody in **1** and **2** above are the beneficiaries or are entitled to the benefit of a power being exercised by the trustee; or

4 any partner of yours or anybody in **1**, **2** or **3** above.

No plc can provide credit to you or a connected person or provide any form of security where credit has been granted by a third party.

What is a credit transaction for these purposes?

A credit transaction is:

1 the supply of goods or land under a hire-purchase or conditional sale agreement; or

2 the lease or hire of land or goods for periodic payments; or

3 any other disposal of land or supply of goods or service for deferred payment.

There are no restrictions on private companies which are not plcs.

Are there any other restrictions on the general rule?

Yes:

1 no company can take over a transaction which is prohibited by any of the rules in **1** to **2** immediately above, for example a company which takes an assignment of a loan contract from the lender where you are the borrower; or

2   where the lender allows the company to take over your obligations under the loan agreement; or

3   no company can participate in any arrangement under which the company, or another group, provides a benefit to a third party who enters into a transaction which, if made by the company, would be prohibited by any of the rules in **1** to **4** above.

This last restriction is a difficult concept to grasp and may be understood by the use of two examples:

- First, a bank agrees to give you an overdraft (a loan) on favourable terms, and in return the company gives its banking affairs to that bank.

- Second, company one and company two are in the same group. Company one agrees to make loans to company two directors in return for company two's making loans to those of company one.

8.4.2 Exemptions

What are the exceptions to the general rule that a company cannot make a loan to a director?

1   Small amounts

A loan may be made to a director of a company or of its holding company provided the aggregate of the relevant amount does not exceed £5000. Note the use of the word aggregate. The aggregate is determined by adding the value of the proposed transaction to any existing transaction with the same person, less the amount by which this has been reduced, and any amount outstanding in respect of transactions with a connected person of the borrower. This is designed to prevent attempts to get around the general restriction on loans to directors by breaking up a transaction into a number of smaller transactions.

How do you determine the 'value' of the transaction?

If, for example, the transaction is a loan, then the principal of the loan represents the value. If the value cannot be expressed as a sum of money it is deemed to exceed £100 000.

2   Minor transactions

A company may enter into a credit transaction with you or provide security for such a transaction if total indebtedness does not exceed £10 000.

3 Business transactions

A company may enter into a minor transaction or provide security for the same if it does so in the ordinary course of its business and gives you no more favourable terms than your financial funding would justify if you were an outsider.

4 Intra-group transactions

In order to ensure that intra-group business is not unduly hampered, loans made by one group company to another are permitted. So too are quasi-loans and the provision of security.

5 Plc short-term facilities

A plc may make quasi-loans of not more than £5000 but you must repay within two months of the company's expenditure.

6 Your expenditure

If you incur expenditure for the company's purposes or to enable you to perform your duties as a director you can claim a refund from the company provided you give full disclosure to the general meeting of shareholders which approves. Alternatively, if not approved by a meeting of shareholders, the transaction is to be discharged within six months of the next AGM. However, if you are a director of a plc your expenditure or liability must not exceed £20 000 in aggregate. For example, the company may make a bridging loan to you where you are required to move house in the course of your duties.

7 Money lending companies

If you are a director of a money lending company then it may make a loan to you in certain cases. Once again it must not be any more favourable than would have been offered to an outside borrower. In the case of a plc, however, such loans must not exceed £100 000 unless the company is a banking company in which case there is no limit.

I am a director in a money lending company or its holding company. What other facilities may I be given?

You may receive a loan to purchase your main or only residence, or to improve your house, or in substitution for a loan provided by a third party for either.

In this instance the terms may be more favourable than would be offered to an outside borrower provided the loan is made in the ordinary course of business and is of a type usually made by the company, but it must not exceed £100 000.

8.4.3 The need for disclosure

You must disclose transactions involving any loan or arrangement between yourself and the company whether or not the arrangement is prohibited. Disclosure must be at the first board meeting which considers the transaction or, if later, the first meeting after your interest has arisen, and your disclosure must be to the full board meeting and not merely a subcommittee. Your name and the amount outstanding must also be included in a note to the company's accounts for the years in which the arrangement was entered into or still exists (*see* under first example in section 4.8.2).

Are there any exceptions to the need to disclose?

Yes. If you or a connected person enter into a credit transaction, a guarantee of such a transaction or an ancillary arrangement with the company for under £5000 there is no need to disclose.

8.4.4 Consequences of breach

What are the consequences of my breaching the restrictions in relation to company loans to me?

The transaction is voidable by the company unless:

- restitution is no longer possible; or

- you or a connected person or the board which authorised the arrangement have indemnified the company in respect of any loss or damage suffered by it; or

- an innocent third party without knowledge of your breach has acquired rights.

Will I be personally liable to pay for any loss or damage if the company suffers?

Yes, together with any person connected with you or any director who authorised your unlawful transaction. You will also be made to account to the company for any gains which you have made. This liability exists whether or not the company avoids the transaction.

If I took all reasonable steps to ensure that the company complied with its obligations in relation to a director I am connected with, am I still liable?

It is a defence if you can show that you took such steps in relation to the arrangement between the company and a director with whom you are connected. However, if the transaction in question has been entered into directly between the company and yourself, then no defence will be available to you. Those connected with you or any director who authorised your unlawful transaction may escape liability if they can show that at the time they did not know the relevant facts which led to the breach.

Are there any criminal penalties I may face?

Yes, but only if you are a director of a plc. The law takes a tougher line with you by virtue of your holding this office. Both you and the company are criminally liable if you authorise or permit any transaction in regard to which you knew or ought to have had reasonable cause to believe the company was in breach of the law. Punishment is severe. If you are tried and convicted in the magistrates' court you may be fined £2000 and/or face six months imprisonment. If you are convicted in the Crown Court you face an unlimited fine and/or two years imprisonment. The company, however, has a defence if it can show that it was unaware of the relevant circumstances when you entered into the transaction.

The law governing loans to you falls under the heading of controlling self-dealing by directors and this heading also covers your duties in relation to personal or secret profits, interest in contracts and contracts with the company, all of which were considered in Chapter 4 of this book.

Checklist: Directors' remuneration

1. Do you understand in broad terms how you are taxed as a company director?

2. Ensure that you know the circumstances in which you can take a loan from the company – the general rule is that loans are prohibited. Check that any loan transaction is disclosed at a board meeting and in the company's accounts.

9

Directors' service contracts

It is important to understand two things about directors' service contracts: first, that you do not have a service contract with the company merely by virtue of the fact that you are a director, and second, where you are also an employee of the company, your directorship and your rights in respect of that directorship are quite distinct from your rights as an employee. Your rights as a director are primarily governed by the company's articles and your employment rights by the director's service contract.

Do the non-executive members of the board who serve on a part-time basis only and receive only directors' fees need a service contract?

No, one can hold the office of director and not have a service contract in these circumstances. In all other instances it is, however, advisable to have a properly drafted contract.

How do I determine whether I am an employee as well as a director?

Unfortunately, the cases decided on this point are not consistent with one another. Where it is not clear what your position is, the courts are generally prepared to presume an employment relationship if you are required to work full time in return for a salary.

Where you are an employee, the Employment Protection (Consolidation) Act 1978 (as amended by the Employment Act 1982) will apply to your service contract.

What are the principal provisions of the Act as they relate to a director?

These are detailed in the following sections.

9.1 Written particulars of terms

You must be provided with written particulars of the terms of employment within eight weeks of the commencement of your employment if you normally work at least 16 hours per week. This will include remuneration, hours, holidays, notice periods and grievance procedures.

9.2 Notice

The company as your employer must give you notice depending on the length of your continuous service. These periods are statutory minimums, and you must have been in continuous employment for at least one month to be eligible:

0–2 years	:	1 week
2–12 years	:	1 week for each year of employment
12 years or more	:	at least 12 weeks[1]

A longer period of notice may be implied by law if reasonable.

Remember the requirements in sections 9.1 and 9.2 do not apply where you have a written service contract containing all the relevant matters, and your actual notice periods will usually be longer than the above minimum in view of the seniority of your position.

9.3 The service contract

What are the salient provisions usually found in a director's service contract?

These are outlined in the sections below.

9.3.1 Notice

The real significance of the provisions relating to termination is that they determine the potential cost to the company if it wishes to terminate your employment, perhaps because your performance is unsatisfactory. Clearly, the longer the notice period the company is required to give, the greater the potential cost.

When deciding on the period of the agreement, your fellow directors must always bear in mind that they are under a duty to exercise their discretion bona fide in what they consider to be the interests of the company and not of you as an individual. It is not in the interest of the company to enter into a fixed-term contract in excess of five years. It is for this reason that shareholders are afforded the right to approve in general meeting any director's employment contract which will continue for more than five years if the company has no or only restricted powers to terminate (*see* section 4.8.2, point 3).[2] One should also bear in mind the recommendation of the Hampel Report (*see* section 4.10) on this question of notice periods.

How is such approval given?

A memorandum of the agreement setting out the relevant terms must be available for inspection:

- at least 15 days before the meeting at the registered office; and

- at the meeting itself.

What if this approval has not been given?

The company may terminate the contract at any time on giving reasonable notice, no matter what the contract may say.

9.3.2 Retirement

As we have seen in section 2.5, in a private company there is no age limit for your holding office as director. However, in common with any position of employment, your eventual retirement from service with the company must be addressed. Most service contracts will therefore provide that your employment will automatically be determined when you attain a specified age and there will be no requirement upon the company to serve any notice upon you.

9.3.3 Whole time and attention

It is likely that the position you hold in your company is that of an executive director (*see* section 2.1.1). As such you will be involved in the day-to-day management of the company and appointed to the board of directors. To enable the company to obtain to the full the benefit of your abilities, your contract will usually require that you devote the whole of your time and attention during business hours (except holidays) to the discharge of your duties in a loyal and efficient manner. If your company is one of a group of companies you may be required in pursuance of your duties to serve not only the company but also any other group company.

9.3.4 Fidelity

Most contracts will require that you promote the trade and business of the company and group to the best of your ability, knowledge and power. This duty will include a duty to communicate to the company any facts, matters, circumstances or information which may affect the company and give full particulars of which you are aware. Typical examples encompass any misconduct, dishonesty or other conduct on the part of employees or your fellow directors, or group directors, which may adversely affect the company or group.

In addition, you should keep the board or the managing director properly and fully informed of the business and affairs of the company and provide such explanations as either may require.

9.3.5 Interest in other business

During your employment you will not generally be directly or indirectly engaged or interested in any other business without the written consent of the board. This restriction will generally apply even if your other interest is outside the usual hours of work. One should understand that this will not prevent you from holding perhaps up to 10 per cent of the equity share capital of a company which is listed on the Stock Exchange, for example shares you may hold in a privatised utility.

9.3.6 Post-termination covenants

(a) Non-competition

The customer or client base of any company is extremely valuable and in many instances represents a major asset. It is therefore essential that when a director leaves the company for any reason his or her activities be restricted for a reasonable period of time and within a reasonable geographical radius from the principal place of business. It is common to include a provision that the outgoing director should not compete on his or her own account, or accept any employment with any trade or business which is wholly or partly in competition with the company. This restriction will cover the director setting up their own business, finding employment with another company in the same business, or providing technical, commercial or professional advice to such a company. A non-competition covenant will not prevent a director from accepting employment with another business where his or her duties do not relate to the nature or kind of business they were formerly engaged in.

I have heard that restrictions upon the activities of former directors are against the law. Is this so?

Not necessarily. The courts seek a balance between the legitimate commercial interest of the company which the director has left and that director's right to earn a living in his or her chosen trade. Provided a post-termination restriction is reasonable in both duration and geographical radius, the courts will support the same. One should note that the ability to include such a restriction is governed by many factors. For example, if the company's customer or client base is not confined to a particular locality there is little point in inserting a geographical restriction of perhaps a three-mile radius from the place of employment. Alternatively the company may trade in an industry where several other companies in the same business are situated in the same city. Here, a three-mile radius restriction will effectively exclude employment or other activity in that city. In these circumstances the court would not uphold such a limitation. The test of reasonableness will, therefore, vary according to the particular circumstances and advice should be taken in either imposing restrictions upon the director or being asked to enter into the same.

(b) Non-solicitation

Another typical post-termination exclusion will be a provision extending your general duty of good faith (*see* section 4.2). This will prevent a director within a specified time period after termination of employment from soliciting or receiving orders from or otherwise dealing with any person, firm or company who at any time in perhaps the last year of that director's employment was:

- a customer or client of the company; or
- a customer or client with whom the director has dealt; or
- a supplier of the company; or
- a supplier with whom the director has had dealings; or
- an agent or distributor of the company; or
- an employee of the company.

In addition, usually any attempt to 'poach' former colleagues or employees of the director will be forbidden. This is designed to prevent a director leaving the company and then systematically approaching the company's staff who may have been working with that director and offering them employment in the director's new enterprise.

9.3.7 Trade secrets and confidential information

Many companies will, over the years, have invested heavily in research and development of its products or services and the processes, operations and systems which it has devised must be protected. Therefore, most service contracts will include a provision preventing a director from revealing to any person, firm or company any trade secrets or any information concerning the organisation, business, finances, transactions or affairs of the company or any group company. The director must keep with inviolable secrecy all matters and information entrusted to him or her and should not use that information in any manner which may injure or cause loss to the company or group. It is important to note that this duty of confidentiality applies both during the director's service with the company and for a reasonable period thereafter.

9.3.8 Discoveries and inventions

It is common for a service contract to state that any discovery or invention or secret process, modification or improvement which you discover (whether alone or with others) while in the service of the company shall belong to and be the absolute property of the company. This will apply if the discovery is in connection with or in any way affects or relates to the business of the company or of any group company. Such a discovery must be disclosed to the company. A clause in a contract dealing with discoveries and inventions will normally also require you to assist the company in applying for patents or other protection in the UK or world-wide. Moreover, you will be obliged to sign (and appoint the company attorney over) any document which has the effect of vesting the ownership of the intellectual property in the company.

9.3.9 Remuneration

The service contract will of course specify the remuneration that you shall receive for your services. This will include the level of salary and timing of payments and will normally state that your salary will be reviewed by the board at stipulated intervals. Attention here should be paid to the recommendations of the Hampel Report considered in this book and its recommendations on the establishment of remuneration committees (*see* relevant point at section 4.10).

Your entitlement to other forms of remuneration such as commission or share option receipts will also be detailed in the contract and the formula for eligibility of each set out clearly. If a motor car is provided to you to assist in the performance of your duties the contract will usually state that it should be of a size and type to be considered by the board or determined by the company's car policy in force from time to time. The timing of replacement for the vehicle and your duties in relation to maintenance will be indicated.

Most contracts will require the company to reimburse you with such travelling, hotel, entertainment and other out-of-pocket expenses as are from time to time properly and reasonably incurred by you in the course of your appointment (*see* section 8.1).

9.3.10 Incapacity

If you are at any time incapacitated or prevented by illness, injury, accident or any other circumstances beyond your control from discharging in full your duties the contract will specify your position. The total number of days in any specified period of consecutive calendar months in which you are incapacitated will be shown. Normally the company may, by giving notice in writing, cease payment in whole or in part of your salary and/or commission from the date of the notice until the incapacity ceases.

9.3.11 Termination

The circumstances in which the company may terminate your employment forthwith without prior notice will be laid down. This is typically where you:

- have committed any serious or persistent breach of your service contract; or

- are guilty of any grave misconduct or wilful neglect in the discharge of your duties; or

- become bankrupt or make any arrangement or composition with your creditors (*see* section 11.3.5); or

- become of unsound mind; or

- are convicted of any criminal offence whether during or outside normal working hours, other than a minor motoring or other offence which in the reasonable opinion of the board does not affect your position as a director; or

- become permanently incapacitated by illness, injury, accident or other circumstances; or

- are disqualified from holding office as a director (*see* section 11.1); or

- are in the reasonable opinion of the board incompetent in the performance of your duties.

A clause which illustrates your relationship with the company is one which states that if you cease to be a director of the company, the employment shall nonetheless continue unless ended by the company. However, if you cease to be an employee of the company your directorship of the company shall thereupon automatically terminate.

Consistent with your duty of confidentiality upon the termination of your employment, for whatever reason, you will be required to deliver to the company all books, documents, papers and records, programmes and other property in your possession and not retain any copies.

Checklist: Directors' service contracts

The importance of the directors' service contract should not be underestimated, yet many directors in privately owned companies do not hold a contract. As has been seen, a properly drafted contract not only regulates the relationship between the company and the director, it can also protect the business from the actions of a director who wishes to leave and compete with or solicit colleagues from the company.

It is said that the most expensive mistake one can make in business is cheap professional advice. On this and all other topics in this book take expert legal advice from specialists in company and commercial law.

Notes

1 Section 49(1), Employment Protection (Consolidation) Act 1978.

2 Section 319, Companies Act 1985.

10

Resignation, removal and retirement – should I stay or should I go?

10.1 Resignation

Am I free to resign my position as director?

Yes, you can at any time resign your office and usually the articles make express provision accordingly (*see* section 6.2).[1]

This is effected by notice to the company or to the company secretary. Circumstances which lead to your decision to resign might include your disagreement with your fellow directors which cannot be resolved (*see* section 6.2).

If the articles do not make express provision for resignation, may I do so anyway?

Yes, you may always resign (but *see* section 11.3.6).

Can I subsequently withdraw my resignation?

No, once given it cannot be withdrawn except with the consent of the company. This is so even though there has been no formal acceptance.

In what form does my notice need to be?

There is no specified form and a verbal notice given to and accepted at a general meeting will suffice. Such verbal notice is effective even if the articles specify notice in writing – but it would not be effective if given only to your fellow directors at board level because the board has no authority to accept. It must be given to the company in general meeting.

10.2 Removal

Can I be removed from office?

Yes, shareholders may by ordinary resolution requiring special notice (at least 28 days) remove you before the expiration of your office, notwithstanding anything in the articles or in any service contract you may have with the company. This is so whether you are a director of a private or public limited company.

Do I have the right to be heard at the meeting where it is proposed I be removed?

Yes, you must be sent the notice and you may also require the company to circulate to the members your representations in writing.

What is the procedure which must be followed by shareholders if they wish to remove me?

Special notice must be given of any resolution to remove you as a director. This means that the proposer of the resolution must give 28 days' notice to the company of his or her intention to propose the resolution. The company must then give notice to the members of the notice convening the meeting or, if that is not practicable, a newspaper advertisement placed or other mode allowed by the articles, normally not less than 21 days before the meeting.

The company must then supply a copy of the resolution to you and you are entitled to be heard at the meeting. It is important to note that in this instance a meeting must be held and a private company cannot resort to a written resolution to remove you without convening a meeting.

At this point you may require the company to circulate any representations which you would like to make. This right will be lost, however, if your articles contain an express power to remove a director by ordinary resolution and the company specifically acts pursuant to that power.

If you are removed, this does not deprive you of any claim for compensation for damages payable in respect of the termination.

10.3 Compensation for loss of office

What considerations should be addressed by the company before seeking my removal?

It should consider the amount of damages which may be payable to you if you are dismissed. If you do have a service contract, while it will not prevent your removal, it should at least give you a right to compensation for early termination, perhaps dissuading an attempt to remove you.

I do have a service contract. Can I still seek damages?

No.

Clearly any provision in your contract giving a right to compensation could render the cost of your removal exorbitant. It is for this reason that shareholder approval is required to give effect to any contract given to you for a period exceeding five years and where that contract cannot be determined by the company by notice, or alternatively where it can be terminated only in specified circumstances. If such ratification is not obtained, any term in your contract giving a right to compensation is void and you will be entitled only to reasonable notice.

Does the resolution demanding my removal have to state reasons why?

No.

Can the entire board be removed by shareholders by a bare majority of votes and replaced by directors of their choice?

Yes, and this right is very important and must be appreciated by you.

Can I effectively prevent my removal by securing weighted voting rights on any resolution to remove me which may be passed at some future time?

Yes. This is known as a 'Bushell v Faith' clause in the articles.[2] However, the likelihood of your obtaining agreement to such a provision in the articles from the contributors of share capital is slight as they would in effect be accepting a position of permanent minority.

What then is the best way to give myself protection?

The adoption of a director's service contract of reasonable length.

Is there anything else I can do to deter an attempt to remove me?

Yes, but only where you are a director in a 'quasi-partnership', for example where you are one of three equal shareholders where you all jointly manage the company and your two fellow directors conspire to expel you. In these circumstances you can petition the court for compulsory winding-up under the 'just and equitable' ground[3] (*see* section 5.6.4). This right may also apply if you manage what is in nature a partnership and you agree with your co-directors that there should be continued participation in management.[4]

It is essential that you understand that you may in some instances be removed as a director but this must not affect your employment with the company and thus your contract. In other words, if your contract can be performed without a seat on the board (and you are not guaranteed a seat) your removal will not entitle you to damages or compensation. Conversely, if you are appointed as managing director, for example, removal from the board will also terminate your service contract.

What are the usual events after which the law states that the office of director shall be vacated automatically?

1 (a) Removal by any provision of the Companies Act.

   (b) Prohibition by law.

2 Bankruptcy or composition (i.e. an arrangement) with creditors (*see* section 9.3.11, point 3).

3 Mental disorder accompanied by:

   (a) admission to hospital (or treatment under the Mental Health Act 1983) (*see* section 9.3.11, point 4); or

   (b) a court order for detention or the appointment of a receiver.

4 Resignation by notice to the company.

5 Absence from board meetings for more than six consecutive months without the permission of the other directors and removal from the board if a resolution to remove you is passed.[5]

The above will be typically found in most companies' articles but may be added to or subtracted from the articles.

10.4 Retirement

What are the usual provisions in the articles in relation to the retirement of directors?

Most articles provide that a proportion of the directors, usually one-third, shall retire by rotation each year.[6] However, in most private companies this requirement is generally excluded or considerably curtailed, and will usually not apply to a managing director who will normally have a service contract for a fixed number of years.

Remember, as seen in section 2.5 of this book, there is no age limit for retirement in private companies and the terms of that section should be noted in relation to plc directors. In addition, you should appreciate your liability for breach of duty which survives despite your retirement (*see* section 4.9.2).

Checklist: Your resignation, removal and retirement

1. You can always resign from your position of director at any time.

2. You can always be removed from office by shareholders at any time even if you hold a director's service contract. However, the potential compensation you could receive under your contract may deter an attempt at your removal.

3. There is no age limit for your retirement if you are a director of a private company. If you are a director of a public company you must retire at 70 unless the articles say otherwise, or unless approved by the company at general meeting.

Notes

1 Article 81(d), Table A.

2 *Bushell* v *Faith* (1971) All ER 53.

3 Section 122(1)(g), Insolvency Act 1986.

4 *Re: A & B Point C Chewing Gum Ltd* (1975) 1 All ER 1017.

5 Article 81, Table A.

6 Article 73, Table A.

11

Disqualification of directors, and wrongful and fraudulent trading

Who can be a director?

Anyone can be a director unless he or she is disqualified for some specific reason.

11.1 Disqualification

The courts' powers to disqualify directors for unfit conduct are not new. However, it is only recently we have seen the implementation of these powers. When Parliament passed the Insolvency Act 1986 it was to curb the activities of directors who shelter behind the corporate veil of limited liability and who, having put a company into insolvent liquidation, promptly set up in business immediately and begin the cycle once again.[1]

The law is governed by the Company Directors Disqualification Act 1986 and although many provisions are not limited to directors, as a director you are at primary risk of disqualification. Since the Act came into effect, an increasing number of disqualification orders have been made which allow for the disqualification of directors of insolvent companies on the grounds of unfitness. Details of disqualification orders are maintained by Companies House on the Disqualified Directors Register.

11.2 Disqualification order

What is a disqualification order?

This is a court order banning you from directorship and from taking part in the management of a company whether directly or indirectly except with the leave or permission of the court. It includes *de facto* and shadow directors (*see* section 2.1). It does not, however, prevent you from continuing to trade as a sole trader. In other words, disqualification removes the privilege of trading with limited liability but it does not remove the right to trade.[2] The disqualification period can be as much as 15 years. Contravention of a disqualification order is a criminal offence punishable by imprisonment or a fine or both.

11.3 Grounds

What are the grounds for disqualification?

There are several grounds for disqualification. These are discussed below.

11.3.1 Convicted of an indictable offence

If you are convicted of an indictable offence in connection with the promotion, formation, management or liquidation of a company or with the receivership or management of a company's property you may be disqualified.[3] This is to protect the public from someone who does not deserve the privilege of limited liability.

11.3.2 Persistent default of companies legislation

This is persistent default as to filing of returns, accounts, notices or other documents required to be filed with the Registrar (*see* section 1.2.4).[4] Failure to file accounts, for example, is seen as a failure to pay the price for the privilege of trading with limited liability. Isolated lapses in filing documents are one thing but persistent lapses which show a blatant disregard will not be tolerated, even though they do not involve any dishonest intent.[5]

11.3.3 Fraud in a winding-up

If in the course of a winding-up of a company it appears that you have been guilty of an offence or guilty of any breach of your duty as an officer of the company you may be disqualified.[6]

11.3.4 Disqualification when made personally liable

You will be disqualified if a contribution order has been made against you for your fraudulent or wrongful trading (*see* section 11.5).

11.3.5 Undischarged bankrupt

This is the only incidence where disqualification against you is automatic. Remember also that liability for your breach of duty remains even if you are declared bankrupt (*see* section 4.9.2, point 3).

11.3.6 Unfit director of insolvent companies

This is the most common ground on which disqualification is sought. As disqualification orders have become common, the courts have had ample opportunity to review the type of behaviour which renders a director unfit: usually more than one company has gone into insolvent liquidation, the deficiency of the assets is substantial and significant funds are outstanding to the Crown in the form of VAT, National Insurance and PAYE payments. In addition, failure to co-operate with the liquidator if your company becomes insolvent may constitute behaviour rendering you unfit to act as a director.

I resigned as a director prior to the appointment of a receiver, administrative receiver or liquidator. Can I still be disqualified?

Yes, your resignation does not prevent the power of the courts to disqualify you.

11.3.7 Disqualification after investigation

If it is in the public interest, the DTI may apply to the courts for a disqualification order (*see* section 6.3).

Give me some examples of cases where disqualification orders have been made.

A failure to maintain accounting records will attract an order. The absence of regular financial information means that you are not able to answer that most difficult question every director must confront: 'Should I cease trading?'[7]

Failure to provide customers with goods or services for which payment has been made and the misuse of bank accounts will lead to disqualification. Regularly drawing cheques in the hope that the account will be within limits when they are presented is a misuse of a bank account. In addition, 'juggling' the finances by only paying creditors who are pressing for payment and even postponing payment until the last possible minute will provide evidence of unfit conduct.[8]

Excessive remuneration and personal benefits when the company is in difficulties will incur liabilities. It is no defence to say that you are being paid no more than the job is worth, where nevertheless it is apparent that your remuneration package is out of proportion to the company's trading success and financial health.[9] This potential exposure gives further attraction to the establishment of a remuneration committee recommended by the Hampel Report (*see* relevant part of section 4.10).

What are the periods of disqualification?

The minimum period is two years; the maximum is 15. Only serious cases should fall within the 10–15 year bracket. These will include where you have been disqualified in the past. The minimum bracket of 2–5 years should be applied where the case is relatively not very serious. A disqualification order is not necessarily the end of the road and not only is it possible to trade without limited liability, you can if disqualified seek the leave of the courts to act as a director or in the management of a company.[10]

(a) Leave to act

On what basis will the courts grant leave?

You may be given leave if you offer undertakings as to the financial control placed upon you, including the maintenance of accounting records and the filing of accounts, and accept constraints on the personal benefits available to you as a director. Agreeing to the appointment of a solicitor to your board may secure leave.[11]

Is it only individuals who can be disqualified?

No, companies which act as directors of another company can also be disqualified.

What happens if I breach a disqualification order?

This is an offence[12] and you may be made personally liable for debts and liabilities incurred by the company while you were acting in breach of the order.

If I am disqualified, can I give instructions to anyone else in the company?

No. If that person is willing to act upon your instructions knowing that you are disqualified they too may suffer personal liability for debts and liabilities incurred by the company whether they are or are not a director.

11.4 Disqualification by the articles

Your company's articles can impose any particular qualification which you as a board may desire. This ability must not, however, be in breach of any legal constraints, for example sexual or racial discrimination.

11.5 Wrongful trading

This is a relatively new form of civil liability and the courts, on application by the liquidator, can declare a director liable to contribute to the assets of an insolvent company. Application can only be made once the company is in liquidation.

What conduct will lead to an action by a liquidator for wrongful trading?

The courts must be satisfied that sometime before commencement of the winding-up, at a time when you were a director, you knew or ought reasonably to have concluded that there was no reasonable prospect of the company avoiding going into insolvent liquidation.[13]

Will I be automatically liable in these circumstances?

Yes, unless you can satisfy the courts that thereafter you took every step with a view to minimising the potential loss to creditors you ought to have taken. The test is what a reasonable director carrying out similar functions in your type of company would know, and your general knowledge, skill and experience. The sweep of wrongful trading covers a form of negligence (*see* section 4.3).

Does the law of wrongful trading cover shadow directors?

Yes.

The crucial determinant in establishing liability is timing. When did you realise the problem and take action?

Should I make enquiries if I suspect a problem?

Yes, the law imposes a duty on you to make necessary enquiries about the company's affairs once there are warning signs.[14]

How can I avoid trouble?[15]

You must be constantly vigilant and keep a watching brief on the company's performance. Simply reading the last accounts will not suffice. You should:

1   Ensure that you keep an accurate record of your activities both in and away from board meetings, ideally in the form of minutes when sitting on the board (*see* section 7.1.4).

2   Satisfy yourself that your records and those of the company are sufficient.

3   Consult a solicitor, insolvency practitioner or seek other independent advice if in the slightest doubt about the company's prospects. Should the worst happen, the fact that you took this step will evidence your attempt to address the problem properly.

4   If you are certain that there are problems, put your concerns to the board and insist upon a board meeting. This will put pressure on your fellow directors. Remember, never easily fall into the trap of believing assurances from your fellow directors that the company can 'trade out of' its current difficulties. If in doubt, consult an adviser and follow that advice. The law requires you to be neither unduly rash nor unduly cowardly; you must carefully evaluate the situation with professional assistance.

What is the penalty I may face?

A contribution order made by the courts either assessed on the net increase in the deficiency of assets against liabilities since the duty to act arose, or worse, on the depletion of assets attributable to the period after you should have realised insolvency was inevitable. You can also suffer interest on the contribution from the date of the order.

11.6 Fraudulent trading

Section 213 of the Insolvency Act 1986 provides that where in the winding-up of a company it appears that the company's business has been carried on with the intent to defraud creditors or for any fraudulent purpose, the courts may declare someone who was knowingly a party personally liable without limitation of liability.

Fraudulent trading, unlike wrongful trading, is firmly based upon dishonesty and not negligence. As a director you have a duty. If your company is in debt, you must stop carrying on business once the company cannot pay 100 pence in the pound on its debts and when in reality the business is being carried on at the expense of the creditors.

Is there any prerequisite before liability will fall upon me?

Yes, it is a requirement that the company must be in the course of winding-up. However, your company need not be insolvent. It means, for example, that a creditor who has lost money to your insolvent company and who wished to make you personally liable may first have to incur further expense and inconvenience in putting the company into liquidation.

Must there have been a continuous course of fraudulent conduct on my part?

No, the central requirement is that the 'business of the company has been carried on with intent to defraud creditors'. Fraud on a single creditor by a single transaction is sufficient to find you liable.

What actions might constitute fraudulent trading?

If you allow your company to incur credit when you have no reason to think the creditors will ever be paid.[16]

Can creditors of my company be guilty of fraudulent trading?

Yes, your creditors can be party to fraudulent trading if they accept money knowing it has been procured by carrying on business with intent to defraud creditors and for the very purpose of paying their debts.[17]

What penalties will I face if found guilty of fraudulent trading?

You may be ordered to contribute to the company's assets if you are knowingly a party to the company's business being carried on with intent to defraud creditors or for any fraudulent purpose. The amount you could be ordered to pay will generally be the sum owed to those creditors proved to have been defrauded as the penalty is intended to be compensatory. However, a court can include a punitive element. This may apply, for example, if you know your company is trading with an excess of current liabilities over current assets and with severe cash flow problems, and moreover you continue trading with no reason to think the company can pay its debts, and finally you attempt to change the company's name with that of a subsidiary and back again to confuse creditors. Such cumulative conduct will allow the court to impose a further punitive element to the contribution order against you.

Any money recovered from you will be made available to the creditors generally and not allocated to particular creditors.

11.7 Qualification shares

Another restriction on your ability to act as a director is a requirement to hold a certain number of shares in the company. These are known as qualification shares. The reasoning behind this shareholding is that a director should be prepared to have a financial interest in the company whose affairs he or she is directing, but it is not obligatory to have a qualification shareholding. If a company does specify a share qualification for its directors this must be obtained within two months, or such shorter time as the articles specify. If you do not obtain the requisite number of shares within the time you must vacate office and not be reappointed director until you have obtained the shares.[18]

11.8 Disqualified director hotline

The DTI has set up a hotline for information on disqualified directors who ignore the disqualification orders against them. Such directors already risk a penalty of up to two years in prison and a fine of £5000.

Most disqualified directors have been found guilty of corporate misconduct or are undischarged bankrupts. In the last quarter of 1997, more than 250 directors were banned by the courts from running companies. The total banned under the Directors

Disqualification Act 1986 is now over 4800. Labour and business service providers now replace building and textiles and clothing at the head of the table of businesses most likely to fail with the director being banned.

Over the same period the number of proceedings being issued by the Insolvency Service has increased by 19 per cent compared to the same time last year. This means that over 300 directors will be facing disqualification for between two and 15 years.

Checklist: Disqualification of directors, and wrongful and fraudulent trading

1. Do you know what a disqualification order is and the grounds upon which the courts may disqualify you as a director?

2. Disqualification may be for between two and 15 years.

3. Permission to act as a director can be given by the courts and only in limited circumstances.

4. If you did know or ought reasonably to have known that the company is going into insolvent liquidation you must take every necessary step to minimise loss to creditors. Personal liability will attach if you do not.

5. To assist in avoiding liability, be constantly vigilant, maintain full records of your activities and take independent advice when in doubt.

6. Never take any steps which might constitute fraudulent trading – a single fraud on a single creditor will result in personal liability and possible criminal penalty.

Notes

1   *The Report of the Review Committee on Insolvency Law and Practice* (The Cork Committee).

2   Brenda Halligan, *The Register, Companies & Law*, October 1995.

3   Section 2, Company Directors Disqualification Act 1986.

4   Section 3, Company Directors Disqualification Act 1986.

5   *Re: The Swift 736 Ltd* (1993).

6   Section 4, Company Directors Disqualification Act 1986.

7   *Re: Hitco 2000 Ltd* (1995).

8   *Re: Synthetic Technology Ltd* (1993).

9   *Re: Keypak Stationers Ltd* (1990).

10 *Re: Gibson Davis Ltd* (1995).

11 *Secretary of State* v *Palfreman* (1995).

12 Section 13, Company Directors Disqualification Act 1986.

13 Section 214, Insolvency Act 1986.

14 *Re: Purpoint Ltd* (1991).

15 Based on Loose, Yelland and Impey (1995).

16 *Re: William Leitch Bros Ltd* (1932).

17 *Re: Gerald Cooper Chemicals Ltd* (1978) Ch. 262.

18 *See* Thomas (1995) *Company Law*, 4th edn. Hodder & Stoughton.

12

Directors and officers insurance

12.1 Background

Given the potential for personal liability for directors under current legislation, is the limited liability protection still relevant?

Remember, limited liability is a protection afforded to shareholders, not directors. The answer is yes where you are both a shareholder and director unless you do not carry out your duties in a responsible manner.

12.2 Availability

There is a growing trend towards viewing a director as a legitimate target. In the main, actions against you could come from four groups: regulatory bodies, shareholders, liquidators and employees or former employees. It is increasingly common for shareholders to bring cases against directors, especially as a result of problems arising out of a merger or acquisition, or if a dramatic fall in share price is thought to be attributable to your actions.

In smaller companies the two most common reasons for claims against you are unfair dismissal and discrimination. While it is the company that is the employer for the purpose of any proceedings, you nonetheless may be named in the action.

You are most at risk when your company becomes insolvent (*see* sections 11.5 and 11.6). Liquidators are often under pressure from liquidation committees consisting of creditors to take action against you if you fail to 'pull the plug' early enough and continue to trade even though you know or should have known the company is insolvent.[1]

Can I insure myself for legal liability I may suffer personally as a director?

Yes. Although it has been possible for many years to insure the personal legal liability of directors and officers in the company it is only since the enactment of s 137, Companies Act 1989, that the enforceability of such insurance has become clear. A company can now purchase and maintain what is known as directors and officers insurance for its officers.

What do I need to check before seeking such cover?

It is essential to check the company's memorandum and articles for the requisite authority. If they do not provide that authority it will be necessary to pass a special resolution (*see* section 7.2.2(e)) to amend the articles to enable insurance against liability to be purchased, as otherwise the accusation could be made that you are in breach of your duties in allowing company funds to be used for your own benefit.

Moreover, you must consider whether you have capacity to vote on the question of purchase of insurance as this may constitute an interest in a contract with the company (*see* section 4.9.1). If you are uncertain of your position you should consult a solicitor.

Who will be covered by insurance?

Directors and officers liability insurance will protect all past, present and future directors and officers of the company. It is important to note that usually this will include *de facto* and shadow directors in addition to those formally appointed to the board. However, certain insurance companies restrict cover to those officers 'engaged or appointed' only and thus *de facto* and shadow directors could be excluded.

Will the company auditors be included?

No.

I am a director of a parent company in a group. Can I be insured in respect of any office I may also hold in a subsidiary or associated company?

Yes, it is common for cover to be provided for the whole group which will be in the name of the ultimate holding company. However, cover for an associate company must be specifically requested under an outside board extension.

I am a director in a group but also hold a 'representative' office in a company outside the group. Can I also seek cover for that position?

Yes, most insurance companies providing directors and officers insurance will extend the scheme to cover this arrangement.

How is indemnity provided?

Usually to you and your fellow directors and officers as individuals collectively. This is where you cannot obtain an indemnity from the company. However, the company is also provided cover where it reimburses you for indemnity actually and lawfully provided to you.

12.3 Cover provided

What will directors and officers insurance indemnify me for?

The typical indemnity will be in respect of your personal liability or to third parties for damages and the claimants' costs as well as for costs of your representation and defence in any civil or criminal proceedings, or costs attendant to any investigation into the affairs of the company.

In addition, you have a clear responsibility to make certain that termination of employment is dealt with in a fair and consistent manner.

The best protection will always remain to avoid litigation and you should consider the purchase of insurance cover in the wider context of identifying and managing potential risk.[4]

12.4 Taxation treatment

How is directors and officers insurance treated for tax purposes?

Payments in respect of qualifying contracts of insurance against your liability made by the company are no longer taxed as a benefit in kind.[5]

However, 'qualifying contracts of insurance' must not:

- be connected with another contract;

- entitle you to a benefit or payment to which a significant part of the premium is reasonably attributable;

- exceed two years, although they may be renewed.

This relief from tax openly applies to 'qualifying liabilities' which are liabilities arising from your acts or omissions in the performance of the duties of your office, or in relation to proceedings based upon an officer's liability for such acts or omissions.

Are uninsured 'qualifying liabilities' exempt from income tax?

Yes, provided that when paid by the company they are liabilities for which insurance cover can be obtained. For example, as referred to above, criminal liability is excluded.

Is the company entitled to tax relief in respect of all premiums or indemnity borne by it?

Yes.

It should be noted, however, that the Inland Revenue appear to be taking a very tough approach towards the availability of tax relief.

What are the key aspects of the Revenue's guidance?[6]

- In group companies it does not matter if you, as a director of one company, are indemnified or provided with insurance cover in respect of that directorship by another group company. For tax purposes the source of pay and the deduction is the directorship concerned, and so there should be no problem claiming one against the other.

- The normal Schedule E rules on timing apply so that a deduction can only be claimed against the pay of the tax year in which the premium or liability was paid. There is no provision for any carry-forward or back as a capital loss.

- There is no provision for apportioning the premium between qualifying and non-qualifying risks and even a minor non-qualifying element will mean no relief for any of the premium.

The tax treatment of directors and officers insurance is likely to be subject to constant review and it is suggested that you seek the advice of your auditors on the issue when seeking insurance.

As a director you face growing exposure to personal liability and effective and comprehensive indemnity should be considered. Cover is readily available and directors and officers insurers are progressively widening the scope of cover to meet this need.

Checklist: Directors and officers insurance

1. As a director you face increasing exposure to legal action by shareholders, employees and regulatory bodies. Insurance is available.

2. Check the extent of cover provided carefully. While certain risks are excluded, it is possible to negotiate the removal of some exclusions.

3. It is important to appreciate that any indemnity you secure with a specialist directors and officers insurance company in no way diminishes your responsibilities as director.

4. Insurers are progressively widening the scope of cover to meet the growing risks you face.

Notes

1 *Under Pressure*, John Batch.

2 *Under Pressure*, John Batch.

3 *Under Pressure*, John Batch.

4 *Under Pressure*, John Batch.

5 Finance Act 1995, inserting new s 201AA, Income and Corporation Taxes Act 1988.

6 *Institute of Directors News*, October 1995.

I am extremely grateful to John Batch who is a specialist on directors and officers liabilities with risk management adviser and insurance broker Sedgwick UK for his kind help in the preparation of this chapter. Thanks also to Laurie Harding of Sedgwick UK Ltd for co-ordinating a very helpful fact-finding visit to Lloyds of London.

Bibliography

Batch, J. (1995) *Under Pressure*.

Drew, C. (1995) 'The Director's Duties', *Gazette* (Law Society), 1 March.

Farrah, J. H., Furey, N. E. and Hannigan, B. N. (1991) *Farrah's Company Law*. (Place): Butterworths.

Halligan, B. (1995) 'The Register', *Companies & Law*. University of Southampton.

King, R. (1994) *Corporate Finance*. London: Blackstone Press.

Loose, P., Yelland, J. and Impey, J. (1995) *The Company Director – Powers and Duties*. London: Jordan Publishing.

Schmitthoff, Clive M. with specialist editors (1992) *Palmer's Company Law*. London: Stevens & Sons.

Sparrow, A. and Gibson, M. (1995) 'Directors' responsibilities – a practical legal overview', *Professional Manager*, July and September.

Thomas, C. (1995) *Company Law*, 4th edn. London: Hodder & Stoughton.

Barc, S. (1995) *Tolley's Company Law*. Croydon: Tolley Publishing.